Copyright

ISBN: 979-8-218-25216-8

Publisher: Forward Hope LLC, Xiomara Ramirez
Chicago, IL

Editor: Floura Lesmana

Illustrations by: Teresa Yu, LCPC, ATR

Photographer: Moises Ramirez

Foreword: Mark Sanders, LCSW, CADC

For permissions or inquiries, please contact:
xio@forward-hope.com

Disclaimer
The information contained in this book is for general information purposes only. The author and publisher assume no responsibility for errors or omissions or for any consequences arising from the user of the information contained herein.

Our Way

to

Licensing

Unlocking Success and Securing the Optimal Job

Xiomara Ramirez, LCSW, CADC, CIMHP

Acknowledgements

This book is a heartfelt tribute, dedicated to the courageous individuals who have embarked on the demanding journey towards licensing as well as those who are currently immersed in it. This book stands as a beacon of unwavering support and boundless inspiration, acknowledging the hurdles faced and the remarkable resilience exhibited by aspiring clinicians. With a deep understanding of the obstacles encountered along this arduous path, its purpose is to uplift and empower each individual, fostering a profound sense of community and unwavering solidarity.

I extend my deepest gratitude to my friends and volunteers who have supported me throughout the creation of this book, especially Juan Hernandez and Tony Pacione. Their belief in this project and their encouragement have been invaluable. Teresa, Karen, Nikole, Marina, Zaineb and Mary for graciously sharing their stories with me. Their willingness to open up and share their experiences is invaluable and contributes to the richness and depth of the content. Their stories will undoubtedly inspire and resonate with readers, providing insights and perspectives that can foster understanding and growth. I am grateful for the opportunity to use our story as a tool to benefit others. Your support and belief in this project have been instrumental in pushing through any discomfort along the way. Thank you for your encouragement and for believing in the importance of sharing experiences.

Floura Lesmana, my heart is profoundly grateful for the assistance you provided me with editing this book.

Mark Sanders, an esteemed model, mentor, and extraordinary leader, generously devoted his valuable time from a hectic schedule to impart invaluable encouragement and profound wisdom.

Teresa Yu, the brilliant mind behind the captivating writing on my website and the striking cover of this book. Teresa, your friendship means the world to me.

Moises Ramirez, my beloved brother, is the driving force behind all of my endeavors. His invaluable contributions include creating my website, designing my business cards, putting together the cover of this book, capturing the beautiful pictures featured in this book, and so much more. I am forever grateful for his unwavering support and talent.

I am deeply grateful and would like to express my heartfelt appreciation to all the contributors who have played a vital role in making this project a resounding success. To my beloved family and friends, your invaluable contributions have made a remarkable impact. While the limited space on this page prevents me from individually naming each and every one of you, please know that your efforts have not gone unnoticed or unappreciated. Your unwavering support has been incredible, and I am truly thankful for it.

Foreword

Finally! A book written to help you navigate state licensure in behavioral health and have a fulfilling career! A colleague was preparing his application to take his state licensure exam. He described the experience as "a nightmare!" During the application process, he had the daunting task of tracking down four supervisors to document his previous work experience required for licensure. He learned that one supervisor retired and could not be located. Another did not keep track of his hours of supervision. This required him to pay for additional documented supervision hours years after receiving his master's degree. In addition, it took months for him to retrieve his college transcript which had to be submitted to take the licensure exam because the psychology school where he completed graduate studies was now closed!

As I write this foreword, it became clear that my colleague could have benefitted from reading Our Way to Licensing book written by accomplished social worker Xiomara Ramirez, LCSW. This book can serve as a guide to help you successfully prepare for and pass your state licensure exam. Topics covered in this book include how to document clinical supervision hours, how to navigate the licensure process in an organized and efficient manner, tips on preparing for the exam, how to deal with test anxiety and stress, and test-taking strategies for individuals who have struggled to pass standardized tests in the past.

The section of the book which details how to interview potential supervisors to gauge quality supervision is priceless! People join organizations and leave supervisors. The supervisory relationship is not only required for state licensure, but also the most important ingredient in employee job satisfaction. This book provides a solid blueprint in preparing for a purposeful and impactful career beyond licensure, aligned with your passion(s) and greatest ability to serve. This book goes on to provide insights on how to assess and avoid unhealthy work environments. As you read this book, you will read and hear the stories of other professionals and how they approached state licensure and their career.

Many of us doing work in behavioral health consider this work to be "a calling." If you feel called to do this work, Our Way to Licensing is the book for you! This book can cut months, even years, off your learning curve. I give the book my highest recommendation.

Mark Sanders, LCSW, CADC
NAADAC Enlightenment Award Winner.
Four Time Lifetime Award Recipient.

Contents

Introduction

Whether you are starting or finishing graduate school, or you are on your way to beginning supervision, this book is for you! As you prepare to embark on the exciting transition into the professional world, one significant milestone awaits you: the licensing process. With "Our Way to Licensing," I am delighted to present a book that aims to equip you with invaluable insights and guidance gleaned from my personal experiences as well as those of others who have navigated the licensing journey or are currently on a path towards licensure.

Recognizing the value of time in our fast-paced world, I have dedicated careful attention to crafting this book with clinicians like you in mind. Its meticulous design considers your demanding schedule, offering a compact size and deliberate brevity that gets straight to the point. Each chapter is intentionally concise, enabling effortless reading and comprehension. While Chapters 1 and 6 may be the longest, their significance will become apparent as you delve into the content.

The primary objective of this resource is to offer practical insights and constructive advice, addressing the unique challenges we encounter in our careers while keeping our unwavering focus on our mission of helping others. This book serves as an efficient learning tool, ideal for busy clinicians like yourself who seek both expediency and valuable information to enrich their journey to licensure.

Overview

"Our Way to Licensing" emerged from my personal experiences as a Clinical Director and my own personal journey in the field. Having navigated the challenging path to licensure myself, I intimately understand the obstacles and uncertainties that aspiring clinicians face.

Throughout my career as a Clinical Director, I have witnessed the unchanged landscape of internships, supervision, and the arduous journey to licensure. This unique perspective has provided me with valuable insights into the struggles and roadblocks that graduates and newcomers in the field encounter. It became clear to me that there was a scarcity of information and preparedness that often hindered their progress.

Motivated by these observations and drawing from my own personal journey, I felt compelled to address these issues and create a resource that would empower aspiring clinicians. "Our Way to Licensing" serves as a guidebook, equipping readers with the necessary knowledge and skills to triumph over challenges and thrive on their own path to licensure.

❖ *Integrity walks alongside self-respect.*

❖ *Confidence walks alongside self-esteem.*

❖ *Resilience walks alongside strength.*

Chapter 1: The Starting Line

In this chapter, I will provide a glimpse into my personal experience after completing graduate school and delve into the transitional phase from graduate school to employment, along with the accompanying challenges. Upon graduation, I found myself ill-prepared and thrown into the professional world. Although I had performed well in the interview process, I hadn't received adequate information or guidance on what to expect in my new role. I must admit that I had solely focused on preparing for potential interview questions, neglecting to inquire about the employer's preparedness for my arrival. As a result, I realized the significance of the interview process, which is why it occupies the longest chapter in the book.

Reflecting on my interview experiences after grad school, I vividly recall the early interviews where my focus was primarily on trivial concerns such as work hours, weekends, and caseload. Unfortunately, in my eagerness to secure a job, I failed to address the more critical aspects of the positions I was pursuing. It was only after successfully securing a job that I began to realize some significant drawbacks.

To my disappointment, it took me six months to realize that the salary I was receiving was below the average for professionals in my field. This revelation left me feeling disheartened and undervalued, as I had invested significant time and effort into my education and expected fair compensation for my skills and expertise. It became clear to me that fair compensation is not just a matter of financial stability but also a measure of professional recognition and worth.

Furthermore, I soon discovered that my initial job did not provide a qualified clinical supervisor, a crucial figure necessary for my professional growth and development. Without a knowledgeable and supportive clinical supervisor, I found myself lacking guidance and mentorship, which are essential for honing my skills and advancing in my field. This realization highlighted the significance of having a supportive and experienced professional who can provide guidance, feedback, and mentorship to help shape a fulfilling and successful career.

These experiences served as important lessons for me, emphasizing the importance of considering not only the immediate concerns during the interview process but also the long-term factors that contribute to professional satisfaction and growth. It became clear to me that aspects such as fair compensation and the presence of a supportive clinical supervisor are integral to building a rewarding career in my chosen field.

After a year, I made the difficult decision to transition to a different agency that provided the much-needed supervision I required. However, this new experience presented its own challenges. I found myself navigating the guidance of four supervisors, one of whom I never had the opportunity to meet or establish a connection with. This situation highlighted a persistent problem within the field, one that seems to be worsening over time and contributing to burnout among professionals. It became evident that the lack of consistent and meaningful supervision is an ongoing issue that requires attention and resolution to ensure the well-being and effectiveness of clinicians in the field.

In this chapter, we'll stress the significance of asking the right questions during internships/job interviews and standing up for oneself and values throughout the hiring process. By doing so, individuals can gain a better understanding of potential job roles, organizational culture, and opportunities for growth. This self-advocacy and proactive approach are crucial for finding a fulfilling career path that aligns with personal goals and values.

Additionally, we will emphasize the significance of supervision in one's career. Understanding the role of supervision and its implications can be vital for professional growth and development. We will explore the benefits of having a supportive and effective supervisor, including the guidance, mentorship, and feedback they can provide. Furthermore, we will discuss how the quality of supervision can impact job satisfaction, competence, and overall success in the field.

When searching for behavioral health clinical positions, it is crucial to prioritize finding a match with the specific community you aim to serve. Simply applying to any open position without considering this factor can potentially lead to personal dissatisfaction and challenges in your work.

Let's go over some key points:

1. Self-Assessment: Take time to reflect on your skills, qualifications, and interests. Identify your strengths,

areas for improvement, and the type of work you are passionate about.

2. Application Tracking: Keep track of the jobs you have applied to, including the company name, position, application date, and any other relevant details. This will help you stay organized and follow up appropriately.

3. Interview Preparation: Once you start receiving interview requests, prepare by researching the company, practicing common interview questions, and developing thoughtful answers that demonstrate your qualifications and interest in the role.

4. Look Beyond Employee Reviews: It's important to always leave internship and job review experiences on online platforms. However, when assessing a potential employer or internship opportunity, it's equally crucial to look beyond employee reviews. While they should be considered as part of your research, relying solely on them can be limiting. Individual experiences can vary significantly, making it best to give the agency the benefit of the doubt and form your own impression during the interview. Employee reviews often represent extreme perspectives and may not provide a balanced and nuanced view of the work environment, potentially leading to hasty judgments and a limited understanding of the overall employee experience.

5. Continued Learning and Improvement: While waiting for responses, continue to enhance your skills and knowledge. Take advantage of online courses,

certifications, or workshops to stay updated and competitive.

My last round of interviews as an LCSW spanned an entire month. I engaged in various types of interviews, including individual, group, and team settings. It's worth noting that some agencies may exhibit resistance when you ask questions, but it's important not to be intimidated, as you have every right to seek clarification. Remember, you also have the right to end an interview if you sense that the company is not a good fit for you. There's no need to endure a lengthy interview if, within the first 10 minutes, it becomes clear that your expectations don't align with those of the agency. You can graciously thank them for their time and politely excuse yourself.

I distinctly recall my experience with a hospital position, during which I underwent four interviews. The compensation and role were enticing, but it was during the final interview with the hospital director that I quickly realized their leadership style didn't resonate with me. Consequently, I promptly ended the interview and expressed my gratitude for their time. The director's response, stating that I required further training and their willingness to help me find suitable training opportunities, did not sound supportive. Instead, it conveyed an implication of incompetence on my part and suggested that they were doing me a favor by offering me employment. I politely concluded the interview and gracefully declined their job offer. In another instance, I interviewed for a federal position, and within the first 3 minutes, my education was minimized with a statement such as, "you just got licensed last year."

I also recall an online interview where one of the interviewers inadvertently expressed negative comments in the chat without realizing that I could also read them. It was a surprising and uncomfortable situation to witness such unprofessional behavior during an interview. However, I maintained my composure and respectfully addressed the comments in the chat. This experience served as a reminder of the importance of professionalism and respectful communication, even in virtual settings. It reinforced my commitment to seeking to work with a company that is capable of addressing and resolving conflicts and is open to acknowledging and learning from its mistakes.

In another instance, during an interview, I faced a disheartening situation where one of the interviewers questioned my English proficiency due to my accent. They went on to state that they had a hard time understanding me and expressed doubts about my ability to conduct therapy effectively.

It is critical to observe the dynamics of the interview to help you gather valuable information and make an informed decision about the agency and supervisor that will best support your professional growth and development. It's important to remember that the hiring process is a two-way street. While you are seeking a job opportunity and a suitable supervisor, the agency is also looking for a qualified clinician to join their team. Both parties have specific needs and expectations that should be addressed during the interview process. Recognizing that the agency needs you as much as you need them can empower you to approach the interview with confidence and a sense of value.

During the interview, in addition to asking questions, take the time to highlight your strengths, share your professional goals, and discuss how you can contribute to the agency's mission and objectives. Demonstrating your potential as an asset to the organization can establish yourself as a strong candidate and negotiate terms that align with your career aspirations. Remember, the interview process is a mutual assessment. It's not only about proving your worth to the agency but also evaluating whether the agency is a good fit for you.

Consider factors such as the agency's values, work culture, opportunities for growth, and the support they can provide to help you thrive as a clinician. Ask about the challenges the agency may be facing. Assess for transparency. By approaching the interview as a collaborative conversation, you can ensure that both your needs and the agency's needs are addressed, ultimately leading to a successful and fulfilling professional partnership.

Let's go over some key points:

1. Observe the Dynamics: Pay attention to the dynamics among the interviewers. Are they coordinated, prepared, and working together as a team, or are they simply pretending to do so? This observation can provide insights into the agency's culture and how well they collaborate.

2. Emphasize the Supervisor and Assess: Remember that in addition to being hired as a clinician, you also need a supervisor. During the interview, expect questions about your qualities as a therapist, but also prioritize asking about the qualities and experience of your potential supervisor. It is crucial to gauge an agency's stance on supervision and their commitment to supporting it. While some agencies may not believe in or actively promote supervision, others may be upfront about not providing it. This part is crucial to the licensing process and allows you to make an informed decision about whether the agency's approach aligns with your own needs and expectations.

3. Request a Second Interview: If the supervisor is not present during the initial interview, it's essential to request a second interview specifically with the supervisor. This will allow you to have a direct conversation, ask relevant questions, and assess the supervisor's suitability for your needs.

4. Inquire About Licensure and Experience: When seeking a supervisor, it is important to inquire about their licensure status and ensure that their credentials qualify them to supervise you. Feel free to ask them about the duration of their licensure, as certain licenses may require a minimum number of years of experience. Additionally, inquire about their experience in supervising others, what their preferred leadership style is, and how much knowledge there is around trauma-informed supervision. This information will help you gauge their expertise and ability to support your professional growth.

11

5. Agency Tenure and Supervision Load: To gather important information, inquire about the duration of the supervisor's tenure at the agency. This will provide insights into the stability and continuity of their role. Additionally, ask about the supervisor's current caseload, including the number of individuals they currently supervise. Understanding their workload will help you assess whether they can offer sufficient attention and support to meet your needs.

6. Inquire About Supervision Contracts and Forms: Request permission to review the supervision contract and forms. These documents will provide insights into the structure, expectations, and guidelines for the supervision process. Reviewing them can help you ensure that your needs and requirements align with the agency's policies.

7. Track Hours and Assess Agency Structure: Inquire about how your supervision hours will be tracked and whether the agency has a structured system in place for this process. Gaining clarity on how your hours will be documented and monitored ensures compliance with licensing requirements and sets clear expectations.

8. Team Interview: Request for a team interview might help you decide. The presence of the team that you will be working with allows you to identify a range of experiences and can be an indicator of a sense of teamwork and collaboration within the agency, which is essential to your professional growth. Understanding the agency's approach to teamwork

can help you assess whether it aligns with your preferences and working style.

9. Agency Recognition of Obtained Degree: During salary discussions, it's crucial to assess whether the agency values and acknowledges the educational background and qualifications you bring to the position. Ensure that the salary being offered aligns with the level of education and expertise required for the role.

10. Consideration of State-specific Factors: Salary ranges can vary significantly depending on the location and state in which you'll be working. It's important to research and understand the average salary range for your degree and field in the specific state where the agency operates.

11. Overall Compensation Package: Remember to consider the entire compensation package, including benefits, bonuses, retirement plans, healthcare coverage, and other perks. While salary is an important aspect, a comprehensive compensation package can significantly contribute to your overall job satisfaction and financial well-being. A good benefit package also serves as an indicator of how much an employer values and invests in its staff.

12. Room for Growth: Assess the agency's willingness to provide opportunities for salary growth and advancement. Inquire about the potential for salary increases based on performance, additional certifications or degrees, cost of living, and years of experience. Keep in mind that initial salary

negotiations may provide a starting point for future discussions as you progress in your career.

Remember, while salary is an important consideration, it should not be the sole determining factor in accepting a job offer. Consider the overall fit of the agency, opportunities for growth, work-life balance, and the potential for professional development. By considering these factors alongside salary, you can make a well-rounded decision that aligns with your career goals and aspirations.

Once you have been hired for a position, there are several important aspects to consider and review.

Let's go over some key points:

1. Job Expectations and Responsibilities: Take the time to review and fully understand your job expectations and responsibilities. Clarify any ambiguities or uncertainties with your supervisor or HR department. This will help you set clear goals and perform your duties effectively.

2. Compensation and Benefits: Review your compensation package, including salary, benefits, and any additional perks or allowances. Familiarize yourself with the benefits offered, such as healthcare coverage, retirement plans, vacation time, and professional development opportunities.

3. Supervision Arrangements: Confirm the details of your supervision arrangements. Understand who your supervisor will be, their experience and availability,

and the frequency and format of supervision sessions. Clarify any expectations or requirements related to supervision hours and documentation.

4. Organizational Policies and Procedures: Familiarize yourself with the organization's policies and procedures, including the code of conduct, confidentiality guidelines, documentation protocols, and any specific rules or regulations related to your role.

5. Professional Development Opportunities: Inquire about the organization's commitment to professional development and whether there are stipends available for continuous growth and learning. Explore whether there are opportunities for continuing education, workshops, conferences, or mentorship programs. A supportive organization that values your growth will provide avenues for expanding your knowledge and skills.

6. Workplace Culture: Observe and assess the workplace culture and dynamics. Pay attention to how colleagues interact, the level of support and collaboration, and the overall atmosphere. A positive and supportive workplace culture can contribute to job satisfaction and professional growth.

7. Performance Expectations: Understand how your performance will be evaluated and the criteria used to assess your progress. Discuss with your supervisor any specific performance goals or milestones that you should strive to achieve. Regular feedback and

performance evaluations are crucial for ongoing improvement and career advancement.

8. Work-life Balance: Understand the expectations regarding work hours, remote work options, flexibility, and time off. Assess whether the organization supports a healthy work-life balance, which is essential for overall well-being and job satisfaction.

By thoroughly reviewing these aspects, you can ensure that you have a clear understanding of your role, expectations, and the support available to you within the organization. This knowledge will enable you to navigate your new position more effectively and make informed decisions regarding your career development. Indeed, having a committed, competent, and qualified supervisor is crucial for your professional growth and development.

As you get to know your clinical supervisor, it's essential to recognize that some agencies may place significant demands on clinical supervisors. Prioritizing the quality of clinical supervision you receive is crucial. Here are some important qualities to look for in an effective clinical supervisor.

Let's go over some key points:

1. Consistency: A good supervisor demonstrates consistency in their availability, support, and guidance. They are reliable and maintain regular supervision sessions, providing you with a stable foundation for your professional development.

2. Focus on the Supervisee: A good supervisor prioritizes your growth and well-being. They create an environment where your needs, challenges, and caseload are the central focus. They provide guidance tailored to your specific circumstances and offer valuable insights to enhance your clinical practice.

3. Adherence to Ethics: A good supervisor upholds and models ethical behavior and professionalism. They demonstrate a strong understanding of the relevant code of ethics and ensure that their guidance aligns with ethical principles and guidelines.

4. Efficient Exploration and Questioning: A good supervisor encourages critical thinking and helps you explore different perspectives. They ask thoughtful and probing questions to deepen your understanding of clinical diagnoses, treatment approaches, and ethical considerations.

5. Provides a Safe Space: A good supervisor creates a safe and non-judgmental space for open dialogue and reflection. They foster an environment where you can freely discuss challenges, seek guidance, and share concerns without fear of retribution.

If you consistently feel anxious or nervous about supervision, it may indicate a lack of proper support. Good supervision should empower and equip you to handle challenging situations. If your concerns about poor supervision persist despite voicing them, it may be necessary to consider other job opportunities. Document your concerns in supervision forms or performance reviews and express your desire for better supervision during future meetings. Prioritize your professional growth by seeking effective supervision to enhance your clinical skills and confidence as a therapist.

The quality of supervision plays a vital role in job satisfaction within a clinical role. Effective and supportive supervision directly impacts your professional growth, development, and overall satisfaction. When supervision is of high quality, you receive guidance, feedback, and resources that empower you to excel in your role. It provides a safe space to discuss challenges, gain new perspectives, and enhance your clinical skills.

Additionally, supportive supervision fosters a sense of validation, encouragement, and confidence, enabling you to navigate complex clinical situations with greater ease. Conversely, poor supervision can lead to frustration, feelings of inadequacy, and hinder your professional growth. It is essential to prioritize and advocate for quality supervision to create a positive and enriching work environment.

Let's go over some key points:

1. Skill Development and Growth: A good supervisor provides guidance, feedback, and opportunities for learning. They offer insights, share best practices, and help you enhance your clinical expertise. When you receive quality supervision that supports your professional growth, it can contribute to a sense of fulfillment and job satisfaction.

2. Promotes Self-care and Well-being: A supportive supervisor actively encourages and promotes self-care

18

and well-being. They recognize the importance of maintaining a healthy work-life balance and provide guidance on strategies for self-care. Having a supervisor who prioritizes your self-care and well-being can greatly contribute to your overall job satisfaction and performance.

3. Clear Expectations and Feedback: A good supervisor provides clear expectations, goals, and performance feedback. They help you understand what is expected of you and provide constructive feedback to improve your clinical practice. When expectations are communicated effectively, and feedback is provided in a supportive manner, it enhances job satisfaction by fostering a sense of clarity and growth.

4. Recognition and Appreciation: A quality supervisor recognizes and appreciates your efforts and achievements. They acknowledge your hard work and the positive impact you have as a clinician. Feeling recognized and appreciated for your contributions contributes to job satisfaction and boosts motivation and engagement.

5. Guidance in Challenging Situations: A skilled supervisor helps you navigate complex cases, ethical dilemmas, and challenging situations. They offer guidance, explore different perspectives, and help you make informed decisions. Having a supportive supervisor during difficult times enhances job satisfaction by providing reassurance, expertise, and a sense of professional guidance.

Supervisors who prioritize professional growth, provide support, set clear expectations, offer constructive feedback, acknowledge efforts, and guide through challenges greatly enhance the professional journey and foster job satisfaction. It's important to recognize that supervisors, like everyone else, have areas for improvement, but what truly matters is their willingness to accept feedback and engage in continuous self-improvement. Remember, effective supervision is a collaborative process that requires ongoing communication, mutual respect, and a shared commitment to growth and development. By actively embracing constructive feedback and remaining open to improvement, supervisors can continuously enhance their skills and provide a supportive and enriching supervisory experience.

Wishing you the best of luck in your interview process and supervisory experience!

❖ *Forgiveness walks alongside healing.*

❖ *Creativity walks alongside new possibilities.*

❖ *Gratitude walks alongside contentment.*

Chapter 2: Navigating the Requirements

Through my own experiences, I've gleaned valuable insights into streamlining the process of applying for licenses or certifications like Licensed Social Worker (LSW), Licensed Clinical Social Worker (LCSW), Certified Alcohol and Drug Counselor (CADC), Certified Integrative Mental Health Provider (CIMHP), and Perinatal Mental Health Certified (PMH-C).

The challenges encountered while navigating my first application process—from identifying the correct forms to obtaining transcripts and coordinating with educational institutions—underscored the significance of meticulous research and effective organization. Learning from this, for subsequent applications, I took proactive steps such as researching requirements first, printing multiple copies of forms, thoroughly reviewing the requirements, and utilizing sticky notes for guidance. I adopted a strategy of tackling one task per day, which allowed me to complete my applications well ahead of schedule, resulting in a notable reduction in stress. While the specific methods may vary with each certification, the underlying principle remains the same: a systematic and organized approach is crucial for success in any professional licensing or certification process.

When applying for licenses, it's crucial to understand that each license has unique criteria. To navigate the requirements effectively, break down the process step by step. Begin by researching the specific requirements for your field and locating the application. Gather necessary documents gradually and obtain required signatures. Familiarize yourself with jurisdictional regulations and bookmark relevant websites. Create a timeline and organize your documentation to avoid incomplete applications. I cannot stress this enough: Keep sealed copies of transcripts and gather signatures from multiple supervisors, especially if you're aware of their impending resignations or if you're nearing your departure from the company. Chasing old supervisors has proven to be the worst nightmare for every applicant. Maintain a dedicated folder for licensing documents to improve organization. While the licensing process can be complex, careful planning and organization will make it smoother.

Let's go over some key points:

1. Identify Field-Specific Requirements: Begin by familiarizing yourself with the licensing requirements specific to your field. Each profession may have different prerequisites, such as education, supervised hours, exams, or background checks. Research and understand these requirements thoroughly before proceeding.

2. Accessing the Application: Determine where to access the application for your license. Often, these applications can be found on the official website of your licensing department or regulatory board. Bookmark the relevant websites to have easy access to the necessary documents.

3. One Document/Task at a Time: Gathering the requirements can feel overwhelming, so it's essential to take it step by step. Collect one document at a time, ensuring that you have all the necessary forms,

transcripts, references, or any other documentation required. Breaking it down into manageable tasks will make the process less daunting.

4. Research Jurisdictional Regulations: Understanding the regulations and application procedures specific to your jurisdiction is crucial. Be aware of any specific rules or guidelines that may apply and ensure compliance with them.

5. Develop a Timeline: Creating a timeline will help you stay organized and on track. Set specific goals and deadlines for each step of the application process. By breaking down the tasks over a realistic timeframe, you can avoid unnecessary stress and ensure timely submission.

6. Organize Documentation: Keep all your licensing-related documents in a specific folder or file. This will help you keep track of everything you need and prevent any essential paperwork from getting misplaced. Having a designated space for licensing documents will contribute to a smoother and more efficient application process.

7. Seek Current Information: Always ensure that you have the most up-to-date application forms and guidelines. Licensing requirements and procedures can change over time, so it's crucial to obtain accurate information from your current licensing department. Check their website or contact them directly to confirm the validity of the documents you are using.

8. Take Your Time: Rushing through the application process can lead to errors or missing important details. Give yourself ample time to complete each task, ensuring accuracy and completeness. Avoid unnecessary stress by adopting a patient and methodical approach.

9. Stay Organized: Maintain clear communication with supervisors and colleagues who may be involved in the licensing process. Keep track of their contact information, including email addresses and phone numbers. Establish a system to collect any necessary signatures promptly, ensuring you have the required documentation to support your application.

10. Keep Extra Copies of Transcripts: It's advisable to keep sealed extra copies of your undergraduate and graduate school transcripts. This precaution will save time and effort in case you need to submit additional copies during the application process.

By adhering to these practices and embracing an organized and systematic approach, you can navigate the licensing requirements with greater efficiency. Remember to break down the process into manageable steps, diligently gather all the necessary information and documents, and approach each task with thoroughness and attention. By implementing proper planning and a focus on detail, you can transform the application process into a more enjoyable and less overwhelming experience.

I wish you the best of luck as you complete your application!

❖ *Mistakes walk alongside valuable lessons.*

❖ *Humility walks alongside genuine connections.*

❖ *Self-reflection walks alongside inner peace.*

Chapter 3: The Application Process

When preparing your application for submission, a few additional tips can ensure a smooth process. My top recommendation is to have your application reviewed by an experienced, fully licensed individual, mentor, or trusted colleague. This person doesn't need to be your supervisor; anyone with expertise in the field whom you trust can offer valuable insights.

Understanding the key elements and potential pitfalls of the application is crucial. Educate yourself by reading online resources and guidelines. For example, an anonymous colleague shared her experience with me, revealing that her application was rejected because she used cursive writing and left certain sections blank. The reviewers interpreted these as missing information, which led to rejection. To avoid such issues, ensure your application is organized, with clean writing and no blank spaces. If there are sections that do not apply to you, write "N/A" to indicate that you have reviewed that area.

Navigating the application processes for professional certifications has yielded a spectrum of experiences, each offering unique lessons and challenges. For instance, obtaining my LSW and LCSW licenses involved distinctly different pathways—while the LSW application was fraught with stress and uncertainty, the LCSW process was markedly smoother and offered reassuring prompt responses from the licensing board. In contrast, my attempts to acquire the CADC certification and the PMH-C license were beset by delays and inadequate support. These varied encounters ranged from delayed acknowledgments and protracted communications with the CADC board, which ultimately concluded positively, to a fraught and disorganized PMH-C certification process riddled with miscommunications and costly retests. Conversely, becoming a CIMHP was a notably positive experience, characterized by efficient electronic processes, responsive customer service, and comprehensive training that met all expectations. Each experience underlined the critical importance of understanding application requirements, proactive communication, and the support of fellow professionals, shaping a profound understanding of the complexities involved in obtaining professional certifications.

Licensed Social Worker (LSW): My experience with the application process for my LSW license was notably stressful and challenging. As this was my first encounter with any licensing process, it was understandable to feel lost and confused. I embarked on this journey alone, without seeking guidance, and while my school provided the necessary documents for the application, they did not offer any insight into the comprehensive requirements and steps involved. This lack of preparation left me feeling overwhelmed and frustrated. It took much longer than expected to gather all the necessary materials and submit my application. Reflecting on this experience, I learned the importance of giving myself grace and patience. This was a new and complex process, and it was fair to feel unsure. This journey underscored the importance of seeking support and guidance early on to navigate such processes more effectively.

Licensed Clinical Social Worker (LCSW): Applying for my LCSW license was a significantly smoother process compared to my initial licensing experiences. With prior experience and familiarity with similar forms and processes, I was well-prepared. I had gathered all the required documents well in advance and had established connections with individuals who could provide support and guidance. Because the process did not feel new to me, I was able to submit my application promptly, the day after becoming eligible to apply for the LCSW test. This streamlined approach and preparedness contributed to a reassuring and efficient application experience.

Certified Alcohol and Drug Counselor (CADC): Obtaining my CADC certification involved additional steps compared to my previous experiences. After submitting my application, I needed to complete 70 hours of Continuing Education Units (CEUs) and provide a notarized page for the code of ethics. This process introduced a lengthy waiting period. Initially, my application was not approved, prompting me to fulfill the CEU requirements. After submitting the CEUs, I awaited a second approval, which eventually came through. Following this, I awaited testing approval. Once I completed the test, there was a waiting period for the results before I could receive my certificate.

Perinatal Mental Health Certified (PMH-C): My journey with the PMH-C certification application was fraught with significant challenges and proved to be the most difficult of all my certification experiences. Required by my job, the pressure to navigate the process successfully was intense from the start. Unfortunately, the support and communication from the licensing board were severely lacking. Responses were slow and often unhelpful, adding considerable stress and uncertainty to my experience.

Despite eventually completing the 'required classes' to become certified, my challenges were far from over. After submitting my application, the processing time was excessively long, and my requests for updates frequently went unanswered or were only responded to after substantial delays. Additionally, the absence of a direct phone line for contacting PMH-C licensing staff compounded the frustration and lack of clarity. Ultimately, I was able to qualify to sit for the exam after various periods of waiting for my documents and information to be submitted correctly.

From the start, the first exam presented significant issues. Not only did it lack the material I had studied, but the questions were also poorly formatted, contributing to a confusing testing experience. After failing the exam, I reached out to the licensing body seeking clarification on the discrepancies I encountered. In response, they informed me that I had been unaware of the essential training needed to pass the exam and offered to provide this training "for free."

Subsequently, I completed the training, which was initially described as optional but later discovered to be essential. Approaching the exam for the second time, I still faced significant challenges. The exam questions were poorly written, and many questions on the exam were not covered in the topics provided during the "free" training. This lack of alignment between the training content and the exam questions not only confused me but also heightened my anxiety, making it difficult to answer based on the studied content. Instead, I found myself forced to guess based on the answer options provided rather than the questions themselves, highlighting a significant disconnect between the training provided and the actual exam.

This interaction raised serious concerns for me about the transparency and honesty of the certification process. It seemed not to align with the usual standards I've observed in professional certification processes, which left me feeling uncertain about the straightforwardness of the situation. While I am not accusing the organization of unethical behavior explicitly, my experience felt as though it lacked clear guidance and transparency, similar to what one might feel when misled.

This entire ordeal was not only stressful but also expensive. Each attempt at the exam cost me $500, making the financial stakes high and adding to the overall pressure of the situation. This disastrous experience highlights the crucial need for clear communication and proper guidance in the certification process—elements that were sorely missing in my case.

Certified Integrative Mental Health Provider (CIMHP): Becoming a CIMHP was a positive experience overall. The process involved electronic submission of all documents, and the exam consisted of a straightforward 100-question format. Customer service was efficient and responsive, and I found the fees reasonable. The training required for certification was exceptional, and I have no complaints about the education provided. This was the most technologically advanced application process I have encountered, making the journey smooth and efficient.

These experiences taught me the value of patience and the significance of diligently following up on applications to ensure prompt responses. Receiving a letter or email pointing out mistakes is not what you aim for. Your goal is to receive the positive news of qualifying for the exam. That's why I cannot emphasize enough the importance of seeking someone who already holds the license you are pursuing to review your application. Though it might feel uncomfortable, having a second set of eyes is vital.

Let's go over some key points:

1. Seek the Review and Opinion of Someone Licensed: It is highly recommended to have someone with a license in the field you are applying for review your application. This person could be a mentor, a colleague, or someone you trust. Their expertise can help identify any potential issues or improvements that need to be made. It doesn't have to be your supervisor, as long as they have the necessary knowledge and experience to provide valuable feedback.

2. Embrace the Discomfort of Seeking a Second Opinion: Although it may feel uncomfortable, seeking a second set of eyes to review your application is essential. Think of it as seeking approval for something important you've done in the past. Don't hesitate to ask for assistance—it's a proactive step toward improving your application's quality.

3. Understand Key Elements and Potential Growth: Take the time to thoroughly understand the key elements of the application and be aware of common pitfalls. Learn from others' experiences and identify areas where mistakes are commonly made. To avoid such issues, ensure your application is well-organized, use clear and legible writing, and avoid leaving any information gaps. If a section doesn't apply to you, use "N/A" to indicate that it has been reviewed.

4. Clean and Organized Application: Presenting a well-structured and organized application is crucial. Double-check for any missing information, incomplete sections, or unintentional omissions. By maintaining a neat and complete application, you reduce the chances of misunderstandings or incorrect assumptions by the reviewers. Remember, you want to receive good news about qualifying for the exam rather than a letter or email listing the mistakes you made.

5. Maintain Regular Communication and Follow-up: Establishing and maintaining open lines of communication with the licensing board or certification authority is crucial. Regular follow-ups can ensure that your application does not get lost in the shuffle and that any ambiguities are clarified promptly. In my own experience, especially with the PMH-C certification, a lack of proactive communication contributed to significant delays and confusion. By regularly checking in, you not only keep your application on track but also demonstrate your commitment and seriousness about the process. This proactive approach can help expedite the review

process and address any concerns that may arise, reducing unnecessary stress and waiting periods.

By following these tips, you can enhance your application's chances of success and increase your likelihood of qualifying to sit for the exam. Remember, thorough preparation and attention to detail play a significant role in achieving your goal of obtaining the desired license. These tips will increase your chances of success and minimize the risk of potential pitfalls.

Good luck with your application!

❖ *Awareness walks alongside reflection.*

❖ *Perseverance walks alongside resilience.*

❖ *Growth walks alongside self– actualization.*

Chapter 4: The Examination Journey

Preparing for the licensing examination necessitates careful consideration and planning. By this stage, you should have confirmed your eligibility to sit for the exam. The next crucial step is to choose a suitable time and date that aligns with your availability and readiness. Drawing from personal experience, I encountered multiple attempts before successfully passing the LSW exam, and I will delve deeper into this journey in a later chapter. On the other hand, my attempt at the LCSW exam without sufficient preparation resulted in failure, incurring a cost of over $200. This emphasizes the importance of approaching your licensing journey with thoughtfulness and intentionality.

As you settle into your new job, stay attuned to exam topics that will eventually pave the way to acquiring your license. Familiarize yourself with the extensive range of information required for the exam, as much of it will also remain relevant throughout your career. Building a solid foundation of knowledge and understanding during this preparation phase will not only boost your chances of success in the examination but also provide a strong basis for your professional growth and development.

Ethics constitutes a significant portion of the licensing exam, so it is crucial to have a copy of the ethical guidelines and review them regularly. Familiarize yourself with medications not only for the purpose of the exam but also to better understand your clients' needs in practice. Additionally, the DSM-5 is a subject that requires ongoing attention throughout your career.

To optimize your exam preparation, it is highly beneficial to invest in an annual subscription to one of the numerous apps or programs offering exam questions and vignettes. Regularly engaging with these resources, even for fun, can substantially enhance your readiness for the exam. Take the time to find an app or program that aligns with your learning style and individual needs. Although I was unaware of these options during my LSW process, I promptly subscribed to an app for my LCSW and CADC exams as soon as the opportune moment arose. Should you require any assistance or recommendations for exam preparation resources, please feel free to reach out to me via email. I would be delighted to share the resources I utilized in my own exam preparation journey.

Exploring various study strategies and resources is vital, so conduct thorough research and avoid impulsively purchasing the first study guide that appears on social media or search engines. Start by asking those around you about their preferred study materials, considering factors such as ease of use and enjoyment of learning. Be cautious of study guides affiliated with specific schools, as you want an effective and reliable resource. Based on my experience, I bought two different study guides for LCSW, and the cheaper option turned out to be better for me. For CADC, I purchased two books but wasn't entirely satisfied. Practice tests are also invaluable, so make time to complete sets of at least 50 questions back-to-back periodically.

Managing multiple books and printed online sources for studying can indeed be overwhelming. To streamline my study process for the CADC exam, I devised a practical solution beyond typical organization. I started by removing the hard covers from the books to punch holes in the pages, allowing me to consolidate these pages along with essential printouts and notes into a single, organized 4-inch binder. This method, while extensive, created a compact, accessible resource. I organized the materials into sections based on topics or chapters, using dividers with tabs for easy navigation. Each section was clearly labeled, enabling quick access to specific information without the hassle of searching through scattered resources.

Creating this dedicated study binder minimized physical clutter and streamlined my study process. It consolidated all necessary information in one place, simplifying access and making it easier to focus on relevant material. This approach not only saved space but also reduced the mental load associated with managing multiple books and sources. Having a consolidated binder provided a sense of organization and control over my materials, allowing for easy updates and the inclusion of additional notes, summaries, or practice exercises, which enhanced my learning experience.

As the exam date approaches, it's normal for anxiety and stress to increase. It's essential to manage these emotions by engaging in healthy coping mechanisms. Exercise, discuss your feelings with someone supportive, therapy is important, and remember that excessive overthinking and stress won't contribute positively to your preparation. Assess your sleep and eating habits, identify stressors, and determine if it's necessary to hold on to the exam. Ultimately, only you can decide which option is best for your well-being and readiness. Preparing for a licensing examination can be a daunting task, but with the right approach and resources, you can increase your chances of success.

Let's go over some key points:

1. Assess Your Readiness Before Scheduling the Exam: Before committing to a specific exam date, take the time to evaluate your readiness. Consider factors such as your knowledge of the exam content, the amount of time you have available for studying, and your overall confidence. Being honest with yourself about your readiness will help you determine the right timing for the exam.

2. Stay Engaged with Exam Topics: The licensing examination covers important topics that are not only essential for passing the exam but also for your future career as a licensed professional. It is crucial to stay engaged with these topics, continually refreshing your knowledge, and staying updated on any changes or new developments.

3. Invest in Exam Preparation Resources: Books, videos, podcasts, apps or study guides. Utilizing exam-specific resources can greatly enhance your preparation. Consider investing in reputable exam preparation apps or study guides that provide practice questions, sample scenarios, and a comprehensive content review. These resources are designed to align with the exam format and content, giving you a targeted and effective study experience.

4. Research and Explore: Every individual has a unique learning style. Some people may benefit from visual aids, while others prefer more interactive or auditory learning methods. Take the time to research and explore different study strategies and resources to find the ones that resonate with your learning style, allowing you to absorb and retain information more effectively.

5. Seek Recommendations From Others: Networking with individuals who have already taken and passed the licensing examination can provide valuable insights. They can recommend study materials, share their experiences, and offer tips and advice based on their firsthand knowledge. Their recommendations can help you make informed decisions about which resources to use and which study strategies to employ.

6. Take Practice Tests Regularly: Practice tests are invaluable for gauging your understanding of the exam content and identifying areas where you may need to focus your studying efforts. Set aside time to complete practice tests under exam-like conditions, and carefully review the questions and explanations afterward. This process will not only assess your knowledge but also familiarize you with the exam format and help you manage your time effectively.

7. Manage Exam-related Stress and Anxiety: Preparing for a licensing examination can be stressful, and anxiety levels can increase as the exam date approaches. It is important to employ healthy coping mechanisms to manage stress. Engage in activities such as exercise, meditation, or hobbies to reduce stress

levels. Talk to supportive individuals about your feelings and consider seeking professional help if needed. Managing stress will allow you to approach the exam with a clear mind and better focus.

8. Ensure a Healthy and Balanced Lifestyle: While organic supplements can assist in managing stress, anxiety, and enhancing brain function for exam preparation, prioritizing a balanced lifestyle is paramount. Adequate sleep, crucial for memory consolidation and mental clarity, should be a priority. Furthermore, nourishing your body with nutrient-rich foods supports optimal brain function. By prioritizing your physical well-being, you improve your capacity to retain information, concentrate during study sessions, and excel in exams.

By implementing these eight lessons learned, you can approach your licensing journey thoughtfully, optimizing your preparation and increasing your chances of success in the examination. Remember, the decision to schedule the exam ultimately rests with you. Consider your personal circumstances, readiness, and stress levels. If you feel that waiting and further preparation will benefit you, it's okay to postpone the exam until you feel more confident. Trust yourself and the effort you put into your studies.

Best of luck with your licensing examination!

❖ *Persistence walks alongside achievement.*

❖ *Courage walks alongside personal growth.*

❖ *Authenticity walks alongside genuine relationships.*

Chapter 5: Facing Challenges Head-On

Let me share my personal journey of facing and overcoming the common roadblocks and hurdles encountered during exams. It is disheartening to witness numerous individuals fail their licensing tests, not due to a lack of knowledge, but as a result of testing challenges. By sharing my story, I aim to instill hope in you and provide guidance on how to navigate these difficulties successfully.

I first became aware of my testing difficulties during the General Educational Development (GED) exam in 1999. Despite feeling fully prepared and confident, I was confronted with a whirlwind of physical and emotional symptoms once the test began. I experienced multiple failures in the GED exam, with one instance leading me to walk out of the test, sobbing and frustrated by my inability to manage the overwhelming anxiety that consumed me. Each question seemed to demand an excessive amount of time, and my trembling hands struggled to write down the answers. After three hours of struggling, feeling defeated, I left the exam room.

I vividly recall the moment I left the exam room, feeling defeated and disheartened. However, my despair was met with compassion when a member of the GED team approached me, offering comforting words. Recognizing my anxiety, he urged me not to lose hope and encouraged me to regain control and belief in myself. Determination filled my voice as I tearfully promised him that I wouldn't give up until I passed. Despite the disappointment, I persisted, taking the necessary steps to register for the test once again by submitting the money order and required form.

Throughout this period, I held onto a powerful affirmation: "I can control myself." It served as a constant reminder of my capability to manage the overwhelming anxiety. On my fourth attempt, after repeating this affirmation countless times, I achieved success. That same compassionate man greeted me, radiating confidence and affirming that I appeared ready and destined to pass the exam.

This experience taught me the importance of perseverance and self-belief when facing exam challenges. It highlighted the significance of seeking support, whether it be from compassionate individuals or through personal affirmations. In the subsequent paragraphs, I will share strategies and techniques that helped me overcome testing obstacles, providing you with valuable insights to navigate your own journey successfully.

Years later, I confronted the LSW exam, where the stakes felt higher and familiar fears and insecurities resurfaced. Equipped with additional education and coping mechanisms, I hoped to conquer my testing challenges. However, it took me three attempts before I could finally triumph over the LSW test.

The first failure shattered me, as I had believed that I had effectively managed my anxiety and blamed myself for not utilizing the coping tools at my disposal. Despite the disappointment, I paid the fee once again and prepared for another attempt. This time, even as I found myself repeatedly reading questions, trembling, and struggling with blurry vision, I refused to surrender. I persevered until the four-hour mark, fully aware that failure seemed imminent.

But then, as I approached the exam for the third attempt, I made a deliberate decision to adopt a different approach. I strategically chose a late test slot, granting myself ample time in the morning for extensive preparation. To reduce anxiety, I engaged in activities known to promote relaxation. I listened to positive affirmations, participated in a rigorous workout, and had calming tea. By the time noon arrived, the scheduled time of my test, I had already embarked on a series of actions aimed at soothing my body and mind.

Remarkably, this approach proved successful. Finally, I passed the LSW test, realizing that what I had needed all along was to allow my body to release its pent-up energy and flood my mind with positive affirmations. This experience reinforced the importance of tailoring my test-taking strategy to address my individual needs and harness the power of mind-body connection.

When the time came to face the LCSW exam, I applied the techniques that had proven successful during my LSW experience and added a few more strategies. This time, I discovered the power of incorporating brief breaks into my test-taking routine. During the exam, I utilized these short breaks to visit the bathroom, where I refreshed myself by washing my face with cold water from the water fountain. I also made sure to drink some water. If possible, bringing your own ice water can enhance this practice further. Additionally, I incorporated physical movements to invigorate my mind and body, such as stretching or walking briskly for a few minutes.

These simple practices, which took less than five minutes, made a tremendous difference in managing my anxiety and maintaining focus. They revitalized my energy and allowed me to approach the exam with clarity and composure. As a result, I successfully passed the LCSW exam on my second attempt. I will explain more about what happened during my first attempt in a later section, offering insights into the challenges I faced and how I addressed them to eventually succeed.

I share my story because it is vital to recognize that failing a test does not define your capabilities as a clinician. Instead, it signifies that your body may not have received what it needs to navigate the testing process successfully. If you possess the knowledge required to pass and find yourself falling short, it is crucial to understand that it is not a reflection of your intelligence, but rather an opportunity to establish a connection between your mind and body.

Each of us experiences stress and anxiety uniquely, so it is essential to listen and learn what your body requires before taking the test. Failing an exam provides valuable insight into the interplay between your mental and physical well-being, highlighting the need to address and nurture this connection. By recognizing this opportunity for growth, you can embark on a journey of self-discovery and develop personalized strategies to better prepare yourself for future tests.

In addition to seeking support from peers, mentors, and support networks, it may be necessary to engage in personal introspection and work with professionals who can guide you in focusing on your mind and body. Remember, you have the power to overcome these challenges and achieve success. Throughout my testing journey, I have learned several valuable lessons that I believe can benefit others facing similar challenges. My next exam was the CADC, and I applied all of the strategies I mentioned above. For the first time ever, I can proudly say that I passed the CADC on my first attempt with flying colors. Additionally, I passed the CIMHP exam on my first attempt as well, which further reinforces the effectiveness of these strategies.

As far as the PMHC exam is concerned, I have decided to distance myself from attempting it again due to it being poorly written and lacking appropriate preparation training and resources. Encountering numerous posts on social media that critique the exam's quality, along with widespread dissatisfaction shared online—including concerns that are seemingly ignored and an exam that has not been updated to reflect actual competencies—has only solidified my decision. This collective feedback has made it evident that the challenges I encountered were not indicative of my testing abilities but were due to the inherent deficiencies within the exam itself and the corresponding study materials.

The realization that the certification is more of a personal preference than a professional necessity, along with the fact that it is not mandated by any regulatory body for practicing in the field, nor does it influence billing and insurance matters, has informed my decision.

Additionally, the company that initially required this certification is no longer my employer, which further diminishes the need for this credential. Given these insights, I have shifted my focus away from this certification to concentrate on the practical application of my skills, where I can make a tangible impact without this specific credential.

This experience taught me the value of tuning into my inner voice, which sometimes means letting go rather than persisting out of habit. As someone who usually sees tasks through to completion, making the decision to step back marked a significant shift, bringing me a profound sense of liberation and alignment with my true goals. Now, I focus on applying my skills practically in the field where I can make a real impact, independent of this particular credential. We all possess an inner guidance system; learning to follow it can bring a sense of rightness and freedom to our decisions.

Let's go over some key points:

1. Testing Difficulties: They are not indicative of knowledge or intelligence. Failing a test does not reflect your abilities as a clinician or your level of understanding. It merely indicates that there are underlying factors that need to be addressed to improve your testing performance.

2. Understand Your Body: Understanding your body's response to stress and anxiety is crucial. Each person's body reacts differently to stress and anxiety and recognizing how these manifestations present themselves in you is essential. By understanding your

body's response, you can tailor strategies to alleviate anxiety and optimize your performance.

3. Persistence and Determination are Key: Faced with repeated failures, it can be disheartening and frustrating. However, it is important to maintain a resilient mindset and refuse to give up. By persisting and continuing to work towards your goals, you increase your chances of eventual success.

4. Self-care and Relaxation Techniques are Beneficial: Engaging in self-care activities and relaxation techniques can significantly impact your test-taking experience. Prioritizing activities that calm your mind and body, such as exercise, positive affirmations, and moments of rejuvenation, can help reduce anxiety and improve focus.

5. Seek Professional Support if Needed: While support from peers and mentors is valuable, historical testing challenges may require additional support from professionals who specialize in the mind-body connection. Working with these experts can help you develop personalized strategies and techniques to address specific hurdles you may face.

6. Exams DO NOT Define Your Worth as a Clinician: Remember that a test is just one measure of your capabilities. Failing a test does not diminish your skills, knowledge, or potential as a clinician. Your worth as a professional extends beyond a single exam.

7. Learn From Past Experiences: Reflect on your testing experiences, both successes and failures, to gain

insights into what works for you and what doesn't. Use these lessons to refine your approach and develop effective strategies for future tests.

8. Reevaluate the Necessity of Continued Attempts: While determination and persistence are commendable traits, it's equally important to reassess the necessity of continuous attempts at a particular certification. Not all certifications are essential, and while some may be required for certain positions, others might not significantly enhance your professional capabilities or career prospects. If you find that repeated efforts are not yielding results, or the certification does not tangibly benefit you, it may be wise to reconsider your approach. Reflect on whether the benefits of achieving the certification justify the emotional and financial costs involved. Understanding which certifications are truly beneficial can help you avoid unnecessary stress and focus your efforts on more impactful endeavors that are genuinely required for your professional growth.

By adopting these insights, you can navigate the roadblocks and hurdles of testing with a renewed perspective. It is crucial to understand that success is within reach and that your worth as a clinician extends far beyond any exam result. Embracing this mindset empowers you to approach exams with resilience, knowing that they are just a part of your journey and not a reflection of your true capabilities. Your worth as a clinician lies in your dedication, compassion, and commitment to making a positive impact on the lives of others. Remember, tests are stepping stones on the path to your ultimate success, and by embracing this belief, you can overcome any testing challenge that comes your way.

Best wishes for a successful and confident performance on your licensing examination!

❖ *Patience walks alongside resilience.*

❖ *Empowerment walks alongside gaining control over one's life.*

❖ *Knowledge walks alongside empowerment.*

Chapter 6: Stories and Lessons to Learn

In this chapter, I will delve into a collection of personal stories and experiences shared by colleagues and other volunteers who were willing to open up and share their stories with me. The aim is to bring about heightened awareness and instill a sense of hope. Engaging in conversations with fellow professionals has revealed shared challenges, specifically centered around the daunting processes of submitting applications, undergoing supervision, and facing testing.

These discussions have shed light on the importance of effective guidance for career advancement within our field. Surprisingly, none of the colleagues I spoke with reported that their time in graduate school adequately prepared them for the hurdles they would encounter thereafter. The recurring theme of inconsistent or outright absence of supervision emerged as a significant obstacle, impeding progress and fostering frustration, ultimately stunting professional growth. Through the narratives and insights offered by these individuals, we hope to not only bring attention to these issues but also inspire a collective effort to address them, nurturing a supportive and empowering environment for all who strive to flourish in their chosen paths.

53

Teresa Y, LCPC, ATR

I had the blessing of working closely with Teresa during her journey towards licensing. When the idea of writing her story for this book arose, she found it troubling, as there are moments when words fail to capture the depth of an experience. The notion of depicting her story through art resonated deeply, especially considering Teresa's profession as an art therapist. I am immensely grateful for the drawings, as they have etched Teresa's story permanently in my heart.

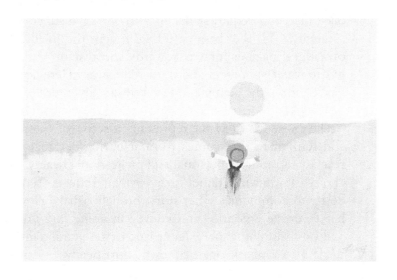

A passionate art therapist embarked on a unique journey to express her story through the power of visual art rather than traditional writing. Determined to capture the essence of her experiences leading up to her licensing, she envisioned the cover of this book as a profound representation of her innermost feelings. The cover artwork portrays Teresa's voyage as a path less traveled, where the footprints of others are scarce. It reflects the notion that her journey towards achievement was an exploration of uncharted territories, often filled with uncertainty and challenges. The path she followed was not well-worn but served as a testament to her resilience and determination.

In the drawing we can see Teresa's artwork, the wheat field takes center stage. The tall grass symbolizes the obstacles and struggles she encountered along the way. The uncertainty of the path is mirrored in the way the grass obscures the trail, presenting her with constant dilemmas and requiring her to rely on her instincts and creativity. As the path winds through the field, the observer's gaze is drawn towards the distant horizon, where water shimmers and tranquility await. Here lies the destination—the culmination of Teresa's adventure.

The presence of water represents a sense of calmness and fulfillment that comes from achieving her goals and reaching a point of personal and professional beauty. The choice of drawing rather than writing reflects Teresa's desire to communicate her story through visuals, allowing her to evoke emotions and convey meaning in a unique and captivating manner. Her artistic representation invites readers to embark on their own introspective journeys, encouraging them to embrace challenges, forge their own paths, and discover the beauty that awaits them at the end of their adventures.

The second picture in Teresa's artwork continues to captivate and evoke profound emotions. This drawing portrays a challenging mountain climb, metaphorically representing the arduous journey Teresa embarked on. Through meticulous brushstrokes, she effectively conveys the physical and emotional aspects of the climb, depicting the sweat, struggle, and determination required to overcome obstacles.

As viewers gaze upon the drawing, they can feel the internal debate that accompanies such a journey. The moments of uncertainty and contemplation, where the choice between resting and regaining strength or giving up in defeat is weighed, are vividly portrayed. These critical junctures reflect the inner conflicts faced by individuals in the field, highlighting the tenacity required to push through and overcome challenges.

Teresa's artwork goes beyond the mere achievement of licensing or reaching the pinnacle of success. It hints at the realization that the journey doesn't end there, but rather, there is more to discover and conquer beyond the initial goal. The painting conveys the understanding that true fulfillment lies not solely in reaching a destination but in embracing the ongoing journey of personal and professional growth.

The seamless integration of the physical and metaphorical climb in Teresa's artwork resonates with the universal human experience of overcoming challenges. It serves as a powerful reminder that life's struggles are demanding and require unwavering dedication. However, through resilience and perseverance, individuals can ascend to new heights and gain a clearer perspective on their achievements.

Ultimately, Teresa's painting encapsulates the profound beauty of resilience, conveying a timeless message of inspiration and hope. It stands as a testament to the rewards that await those who are willing to embrace the journey, conquer obstacles, and persist in their pursuit of greatness. Through her art, Teresa reminds us that the true essence of accomplishment lies not only in reaching the top but in the transformative growth and self-discovery experienced along the way.

Xiomara R, LCSW, CADC, CIMHP

Allow me to share my journey towards licensing, hoping that you can glean valuable lessons from both the explicit and implicit experiences I encountered along the way. Let's start from the beginning, which is my graduate school experience. During my time in graduate school, I embarked on a journey to gain the necessary knowledge and skills to become a licensed clinician. I was filled with anticipation and excitement as I entered this new phase of my education and career. The coursework and training provided a solid foundation, but it was the clinical internship that truly tested and shaped me as a future practitioner.

As I eagerly began my clinical internship, little did I know that it would take me outside of my country of residence. The prospect of an international placement was both exhilarating and daunting. On one hand, I was thrilled at the opportunity to immerse myself in a different culture and work with diverse populations. On the other hand, I knew that being away from the familiar support network of friends, family, and mentors would present its own set of challenges.

I was exposed to a multitude of cases, each presenting its own complexities and nuances. The diversity of clients and their backgrounds broadened my understanding of human experiences and expanded my cultural competence. I became more aware of the impact of social, economic, and political factors on individuals' mental health. However, one aspect of my international clinical internship that proved to be challenging was the level of hands-on supervision. Due to the geographical distance and time zone differences, it was not always feasible to have immediate and direct guidance from my supervisors. While they were supportive and available to some extent, there were instances when I had to navigate complex cases and crises on my own. This lack of hands-on supervision left me feeling uncertain and occasionally overwhelmed, as there were moments when I could have greatly benefited from immediate guidance. The intensity of the cases I encountered during my internship made it even more difficult to find a space for personal debriefing and processing.

The needs of the community I served were significant, and as a result, my own need for emotional support often took a backseat. I felt a sense of responsibility towards my clients and their welfare, which sometimes made it challenging to prioritize my own well-being. In those moments of vulnerability and emotional strain, I sought solace and support through social media. I created an outlet to share my struggles, seek advice from fellow interns or professionals, and find comfort in knowing that I was not alone in my experiences. This virtual support network provided me with a sense of community and understanding that helped alleviate some of the isolation I felt. Nevertheless, there were nights when the weight of the internship took its toll on me.

I remember falling asleep with tears streaming down my face, questioning my abilities and worrying about the potential impact of my actions on clients. The stark disparities I witnessed in the community, such as limited access to basic necessities like food, further added to my emotional burden. I grappled with feelings of guilt and helplessness, uncertain about how to strike a balance between empathy and maintaining healthy boundaries. I won't delve into further elaboration. However, during my internship I experienced condescending and disrespectful comments, such as "use your brain" and "can you think," made by the person in charge of signing my hours. As I approached the completion of my internship and prepared for my final papers, I encountered additional challenges. I struggled to find the right words to articulate my experiences and the impact they had on my personal and professional growth. I yearned for a safe and supportive environment where I could freely express my truth without fear of judgment or repercussions.

Despite these difficulties, I persisted and ultimately graduated, armed with the belief that my journey towards licensure would offer improved support and supervision. I remained optimistic that the challenges I faced during my clinical internship and supervision would serve as valuable lessons, strengthening my resilience and shaping my approach as a future clinician. The experience of my clinical internship, while demanding and at times overwhelming, also provided me with an extraordinary opportunity for growth and learning. It instilled in me a deep sense of empathy, cultural sensitivity, and a commitment to advocating for well-being. I am currently a field instructor for two universities in Illinois and a private clinical supervisor, with the aim of becoming everything I wished I had during my own internship or clinical supervision period.

My first job after grad school was as an Addiction Counselor, and I recall the immense joy I felt during those early days. Eager to learn, I arrived at an agency dealing with a significant turnover, leaving me without proper training. Armed with the knowledge gained from grad school and a few books on group dynamics, I somehow managed to navigate the challenges. However, three months into the job, I realized I still hadn't received any supervision. Despite the promise of hiring a qualified supervisor, which kept me there for over a year, my repeated requests and intentions went unanswered. Within nine months at the agency, I came to the realization that they were hiring program managers who lacked the qualifications to supervise me, let alone manage effectively. After a year and a half, I finally found a job that offered clinical supervision, but even then, it proved inconsistent with frequent cancellations.

The group supervision sessions were far from clinical; in fact, they often felt chaotic and focused more on programmatic matters than on clinical concerns. I vividly remember constantly reminding my supervisor of the code of ethics and bringing up the importance of staying client-centered rather than program-centered. I pushed back and emphasized that the agency failed to deliver on their claims of providing trauma-informed care. As you can imagine, I faced significant challenges during that time. I experienced being ignored, dismissed, and, worst of all, witnessing some clinicians compromising their values to maintain their job or sustain relationships with upper leadership. By the time I reached the 1.5-year mark, I was utterly exhausted.

The toll of the job had taken its toll on me physically, as I gained weight and appeared visibly miserable. I have developed a tendency to resort to stress eating as a coping mechanism. Working for an organization renowned for its excellence, my aspirations of being part of a thriving and wholesome workplace had been shattered. While I knew that private practice was an option, my heart didn't lie in that setting. I had and still have a genuine passion for working with the pressing needs of our communities. After finally completing the required hours, I eagerly submitted my LCSW application, even though I knew I wasn't fully prepared to take the test.

I found myself unprepared lacking both sufficient study and readiness, to face the impending examination, but at that point, I didn't care. I was desperate for the hope that something new and better awaited me. I vividly recall scheduling the first available testing appointment. However, the day before the test, one of my clients from the shelter attempted suicide. In a difficult decision, I had to choose between going home to rest and be better prepared for the test or supporting my client in their time of need. Ultimately, I chose to accompany my client to the hospital and spent the night at the emergency room. Exhausted but determined, I showed up for the test at 8am. However, despite my efforts, I fell just five points short of passing.

I remember the overwhelming mix of emotions I had to endure in that moment. I felt alone even when there were genuine clinicians around me. On my second attempt, I successfully passed the test. As I received the results, tears of joy streamed down my face. Overwhelmed with emotions, I sat down, and the lady administering the results gave me the space I needed before saying, "It's over, you passed. Congratulations." Her words felt like a heavenly message. After obtaining my LCSW license, I was driven by a strong determination to fill the role of a supportive supervisor that I had lacked during my own professional journey.

Recognizing the significance of effective supervision, I eagerly enrolled in clinical supervision, group supervision, and trauma-informed supervision training. It was clear to me that I needed to acquire the necessary skills and knowledge to become the supervisor I had always yearned for. As a testament to my commitment, I am currently listed as a qualified supervisor on the NASW website, ready to guide and empower emerging professionals in their own career paths.

Today, I supervise a team of clinicians. My commitment to them is to provide the kind of supervision I never received and to be the supportive and empowering supervisor that I wished for. In addition, I pursued certification as an Enneagram Instructor, ensuring that my qualifications extend beyond the clinical realm to include a deep understanding of individual personalities. Through this journey, I have come to realize the pervasive need that exists in every setting we encounter. I have witnessed the need within our own field, and it has strengthened my resolve to become the kind of supervisor who empowers and equips therapists to reach their full potential.

Observing clinicians who are struggling or making "mistakes" often leads me to reflect on the role of their internship supervisors and the quality of the supervision they received during their first two years of clinical supervision. The truth is that finding high-quality supervision can be a rarity in the field. It is disheartening to witness the impact that inadequate or ineffective supervision can have on clinicians' professional development and the potential consequences for their clients. The importance of investing in quality supervision cannot be overstated, as it serves as a vital foundation for clinicians to develop their skills, gain confidence, and provide the best possible care. Efforts should be made to prioritize and enhance the quality of supervision to support the growth and success of clinicians throughout their careers.

The truth is, we are all here in this field to support others. If mistakes are made, it is often because the knowledge we gain from books and theories doesn't always perfectly align with the complexities of real-life client-therapist interactions. Recognizing this, I am driven to bridge that gap and provide practical guidance and support to therapists facing the challenges of their work. It is my aspiration to be the supervisor who nurtures growth, cultivates resilience, and helps therapists navigate the intricacies of their profession, ensuring that they can deliver the best possible care to their clients.

My message is: keep your hopes high. We face shared challenges in our field, ranging from bad internship experiences to daunting application processes and inadequate supervision. Additionally, toxic coworkers are a reality in many work environments, and it's often impossible to avoid them unless you work remotely in a private practice setting or in a job that does not require you to work with a team. This topic, however, is broad and complex enough to warrant a deeper exploration, potentially in my next book. Despite these obstacles, it's important to stay focused on your professional growth and the positive impact you can make. Inconsistent or absent supervision hinders your progress and frustrates your growth. Let's shed light on these issues, inspire collective efforts, and create a supportive and empowering environment. Please prioritize quality supervision to develop skills, gain confidence, and provide the best possible care. Embrace the lessons from your experiences, be resilient, and seek support. Together, let's foster a culture of collaboration where you flourish and deliver excellent care. Remember, you are not alone—reach out, share, and seek guidance.

In my story, I shared a compelling narrative of self-advocacy, where I maintained unwavering optimism in the face of challenges and setbacks. This journey served as a testament to the ability to overcome unfavorable circumstances. I emphasized the importance of dedicating time to find a suitable job, as choosing the wrong one can lead to countless headaches. Let us always remember the profound wisdom encapsulated in these words: "You do not have to be perfect to be successful." Alongside this powerful sentiment, another quote resonates deeply: "Success is finding the right job environment for your personality." These timeless words were spoken to me by Anthony J. Pacione, emphasizing the importance of embracing one's individuality and leveraging personal attributes to achieve success.

Mary, MA, CADC

I graduated in 2012 with a master's degree in counseling, but my journey towards licensure has been challenging. Despite my efforts, I have failed the LPC exam three times, primarily due to overwhelming test anxiety and personal stress. As a single mother, I faced the additional responsibility of balancing my studies and full-time employment, which led me to make the difficult decision of placing my son in boarding school to pursue my education and career aspirations.

After multiple unsuccessful attempts at passing the LPC exam, I reached a point where I felt discouraged and gave up on obtaining that license. However, I didn't let that setback define my future. Instead, I sought consistent supervision for my pursuit of the LCPC license, and I am now experiencing the positive impact of engaging with and learning from my current clinical supervisor. Their guidance and support have brought me newfound happiness and fulfillment in my professional development.

Regrettably, the LPC exam was not my initial encounter with such obstacles. Back in 2008, I faced a similar situation when I attempted to pass the CADC license exam. I did not succeed in my initial attempt to pass the CADC exam. On my second attempt, I had to take a week off from work to dedicate my time solely to studying and ensuring relaxation before the test. The stakes were high, as failure would have resulted in a demotion from my position as a counselor at the agency I was working for. The thought of letting down my clients, whom I deeply cared for, motivated me to put in the necessary effort. Building a caseload had been a labor of love, and I couldn't afford to falter. I needed to succeed for both myself and the individuals I was helping. Thankfully, my dedication paid off, and I passed the exam, leading me to become a substance use counselor.

Presently, I am receiving ongoing supervision that will guide me in applying to sit for the LCPC exam. It has been a long and arduous journey spanning over a decade to reach this point. Through my experiences, I have learned an invaluable lesson that I want to share with others embarking on a similar path: Start studying for the licensing exam while you are still in graduate school. Don't wait until later to begin preparing. By proactively dedicating time and effort to studying, you can alleviate some of the stress and anxiety associated with the exam, giving yourself a better chance at success.

My story is one of resilience, perseverance, and the importance of finding the right support system. Despite the setbacks and sacrifices I have encountered along the way, I remain determined to achieve my goal of becoming a licensed clinical professional counselor. And I hope that by sharing my journey, I can inspire others who may be facing similar challenges to continue pursuing their dreams with hope and unwavering dedication.

Karen W, MA, CADC

Throughout my online graduate school journey, I faced numerous challenges. Juggling the responsibilities of studying, caring for my small children, and dealing with an unsupportive husband was no easy task. In my determination to succeed, I even resorted to renting a storage unit as my makeshift office. Grad school itself was a positive experience, but it wasn't until the end that I discovered the need for an internship, leaving me furious and ill-prepared. My first attempt for my license was in May, before I graduated. There was no preparation class for my exam. I knew the basics of how to register for the test and how many questions there were. As far as the knowledge, I was struggling to comprehend all of the knowledge that would be in the test. Being that my class was also on Zoom, it was difficult to meet with my professors after class for a discussion. Most of the time, classes ended early due to the teachers wanting to end class. I think what would have helped me personally more was a class offered—not required—on HOW to take the test. What type of questions it had, review topics, things like that. I had never been made aware I would have to take a licensing test in the first place as well.

When I was given information to secure an internship, I was shocked that I had so few options. The other students had a 28-page book of options, and I had seven sites. With limited options, I managed to secure an internship in a hospital setting, only to face an authoritative, non-native English-speaking supervisor whose communication was both difficult and hurtful.

72

During that internship, I endured a degrading environment where I was forbidden to speak, not allowed to engage with clients, and limited to observing and taking notes. The stress took its toll on me, and eventually I couldn't bear it any longer. I reached out to my teachers, who understood the severity of the situation and promptly removed me from that toxic environment. However, the emotional scars remained, and I shed tears almost daily while my health suffered due to the stress.

Moving forward, I embarked on a second internship, which proved to be a better experience, although supervision was lacking. Despite these setbacks, I mustered the motivation to seek my first job and eagerly started my LCPC hours at a detox center, expecting the support promised during the interview. However, the reality was far from the truth. I received no training and minimal supervision, and when I sought support, I was met with dismissive responses. Despite my efforts, I attempted my LPC exam once again during this period, only to experience failure. It became evident that my graduate school had not sufficiently equipped me for the challenges of the exam.

During my 110-day tenure, I worked tirelessly, running groups and seeing clients, but my efforts were not acknowledged. In my 90-day evaluation, they blindsided me by stating I hadn't learned fast enough or followed directives, resulting in termination. This left me feeling devastated and believing my professional life was over. My mental health suffered, and I took a break. I focused on recovery before pursuing new job opportunities.

During the job search, I learned that discussing my previous job experiences hinder my chances. But eventually, I found a job where I received proper training and felt comfortable. Right before I started my new job, I attempted the LPC exam for the third time, only to fall short once again. To this day, I have a supportive supervisor and lead therapist who are always ready to address my concerns. From this journey, I've learned to never give up and that it is possible to find support and happiness despite adversity. I've realized that being unhappy in our work can lead to hating our lives, and therefore, it's crucial to advocate for ourselves, question our graduate programs, and never be afraid to speak up.

The lessons I've learned from my experiences are powerful and can be summarized in one paragraph. I've come to understand that perseverance is key—never giving up is essential, as it is possible to find the support and happiness we deserve despite the challenges we face. I've learned that enduring unhappiness in our work can lead to hating our lives, so it's crucial to seek environments that nurture our well-being. My message to others is simple: keep trying, advocate for yourself, and don't be afraid to question your graduate program's preparedness for the licensing process. By asking questions and speaking up, we can navigate our professional journeys with resilience and ensure our voices are heard.

A.M, LCPC

I remember embarking on a journey with dreams of studying law. The allure of the legal world fascinated me, and I believed it was my destined path. However, as I delved into the intricacies of the law, I quickly realized that it wasn't the right fit for me. The rigid structure and demanding nature left me feeling unfulfilled and uninspired. With a brave heart and a desire to make a difference in people's lives, I made a bold decision to transition to graduate school and pursue a career as a therapist. The prospect of helping others navigate their emotional landscapes filled me with excitement and purpose. In grad school, I thrived and showcased my abilities as a compassionate helper. However, amidst the sea of success, I couldn't shake off a persistent feeling of seclusion and overwhelm that loomed over me.

During this challenging time, a compassionate classmate recognized my struggle and convinced me not to quit. Their unwavering support and encouragement became a guiding light, inspiring me to push through the barriers and continue my journey in graduate school. As I embarked on my internship, I found myself placed in a transitional housing program, feeling somewhat left out. Despite these initial feelings of isolation, I soon discovered a deep connection with my internship, falling in love with the work and developing a strong bond with my supervisors. Although I yearned to stay and work with the incredible team that had guided and mentored me, there were no openings available at that time. Undeterred, I persisted in my pursuit, and a month later, I landed my first job as a crisis worker. With time, I transitioned into a mental health therapist position within the same company, cherishing the opportunity to make a difference in people's lives. However, the toxic environment in the department began to take its toll, leaving me feeling burned out and once again isolated.

Driven by my unwavering determination, I decided to seek another job and explore the field. It was during this period that I faced my most significant challenge yet—passing the LPC exam. Struggling with debilitating test anxiety, I faltered and failed the exam five times. The weight of disappointment threatened to crush my spirit, but deep within me, I knew I couldn't give up. Fueled by my ambition and with the unwavering support of my three previous exceptional supervisors, I persevered. I continued accumulating the necessary hours for my LCPC application, refusing to let setbacks define me. Finally, after three attempts, the day came when I triumphantly passed the LCPC exam, filling me with newfound confidence and resilience as I joined a group practice and discovered contentment in my work.
Along this transformative path, I learned invaluable lessons.

I honed my ability to read the room, understanding the intricate dynamics at play within therapy sessions. Moreover, I discovered the importance of self-advocacy—recognizing my own needs and asserting them confidently. While the group practice provided a fulfilling experience, I knew deep down that my long-term vision lay in a supervisory role where I could shape and guide other therapists. With my sights set on the future, I continue to grow and evolve. Each step forward carries with it the wisdom gained from my past experiences. My goal to transition into a supervisory position fuels my determination, propelling me forward in my pursuit of making a lasting impact on the field of therapy. As the sun sets on this chapter of my life, I stand firm in the belief that the hardships I faced were not in vain. They shaped me into a resilient and empathetic therapist, armed with the courage to overcome obstacles and the compassion to create meaningful change. The next chapter awaits, and I embrace it with open arms, ready to soar to new heights and fulfill my aspirations.

My message to others is that the road to finding your true passion and purpose may not always be straightforward or without obstacles. It's okay to explore different paths, make changes, and adapt along the way. Embrace the challenges and setbacks as opportunities for growth and learning. Persevere through self-doubt, external pressures, and moments of isolation, knowing that with determination and unwavering belief in yourself, you can overcome any obstacle. Trust in your abilities, advocate for your needs, and surround yourself with supportive mentors and colleagues who uplift and inspire you. And most importantly, never lose sight of your dreams and aspirations. Your journey may have twists and turns, but with resilience and a steadfast commitment to self-discovery, you will find your place in the world and make a meaningful impact in the lives of others.

Nikole G, LPC

My journey of self-discovery began as I ventured into graduate school while balancing a full-time job. This decision was fueled by a burning desire to find my purpose and unlock my true potential. Grad school quickly became a source of inspiration, and I savored every transformative moment, especially the enlightening mock counseling sessions during class. Navigating the demands of grad school, parenting, and a full-time job proved to be a challenge, but I persevered with determination and grace.

Fortunately, my job at the time granted me the flexibility I needed to navigate this delicate balancing act. This invaluable flexibility allowed me to immerse myself fully in both my studies and my responsibilities as a parent. Sacrificing weekends and late nights, I devoted myself wholeheartedly to my studies, driven by the belief that this path would lead me to my purpose.

As graduation approached, the time came to embark on an internship. I eagerly applied to four internships, and to my delight, three of them accepted me. After careful consideration, I chose an internship that understood and supported my lifestyle at that time. Although the experience was fulfilling to a certain extent, I felt a lack of the professional feedback necessary for my growth and preparation for a new career. While I relished the opportunity to make an impact and connect with clients, the supervision and guidance I longed for were not fully provided. Despite this, my dedication to helping others remained unwavering.

Upon completing the internship, I found myself at a crossroads. Comparing salaries in the field, I realized that I was not yet financially ready to make a career transition. I dedicated twelve more years to a full-time parenting role while staying at a job where I no longer found fulfillment. The allure of money began to fade, prompting me to embark on a quest for a deeper meaning and purpose in my life.

To explore this longing for purpose, I turned to volunteer work within my community. Creating a safe space for those struggling with mental health needs became my passion and a profound source of fulfillment. It was during this time that I made the decision to transition fully into the counseling field. In 2017, amidst personal challenges, I triumphed by passing my LPC exam. However, the loss of two significant individuals during that same year dealt a blow to my mental health, prompting me to pause and heal before continuing my licensing process.

Finally, a new opportunity emerged—a job in a residential program. Initially, supervision was really good; however, it lacked consistency. When received, it was good supervision. Over the course of two years, I dedicated myself to accumulating the necessary hours for the LCPC exam and applying for CAADC certification. The journey was not without its obstacles, as submitting my LCPC application proved challenging due to missing transcripts from a defunct university. Nonetheless, after four months of unwavering determination, my transcripts were verified. In contrast, the CAADC application process flowed more smoothly, with an email guiding me to complete additional CEUs.

81

Now, filled with excitement and anticipation, I am preparing to sit for both exams this year. At this moment, I find immense satisfaction in my current job. It has taught me invaluable lessons in time accountability and the creation of healthier boundaries, which have begun to positively impact my personal life. The team I work with is exceptional, providing great supervision and support. Surrounded by individuals who genuinely wish to see me thrive, I feel a sense of purpose as I move closer to establishing my own private practice.

Every experience, every job, and every challenge I faced has played an integral role in preparing me for this fulfilling industry. I made the conscious decision to shift my focus from chasing money to pursuing my purpose, and I can confidently say that the amount of gratification I now experience far outweighs any monetary compensation.

I vividly remember those moments when I drove to work, sat in my car, reluctant to go into work. Although my income may be less, the satisfaction and fulfillment I derive from my work are beyond measure. Reflecting on my journey, I want to share a powerful message with others: It is never too late to pursue your dreams. Even if life takes you on a different path, embrace the opportunity to revisit and resume your passions.

Zaineb A, MEd, BCBA

Grad school was a transformative experience for me, as I had the opportunity to pursue it online. While it was a decent journey, I knew that to truly excel in my field, I needed practical experience. This led me to choose an internship at an agency that catered to individuals with autism, where I was already working at the time. Little did I know that this internship would bring both rewarding experiences and unexpected challenges.

Unfortunately, during my time at the agency, I faced instances of racism due to my identity as a Muslim Arab woman who wore a hijab. This discrimination made me realize the importance of diversity, inclusion, and creating a safe space for everyone. Despite these hardships, I remained committed to my work and used the experience as fuel to become an advocate for equality within the field.

Throughout my internship, I noticed a lack of proper supervision. My supervisor, although friendly, seemed more laid-back than she should have been. Our meetings were often casual and lacked the necessary structure and guidance. Looking back, I understand that a solid support system and regular, focused supervision are crucial for professional growth. However, despite the challenges, I developed strong clinical skills through my dedication and the support of my coworkers.

The application process for licensure was surprisingly straightforward for me. I was fortunate to navigate through it with relative ease, which allowed me to focus on my studies and prepare for the next steps in my career.

When the time came to take the licensure exam, I dedicated myself to thorough preparation. I put in the necessary time and effort to ensure I had a solid understanding of the material. As a result of my hard work and determination, I was able to pass the exam on my first attempt. It was an exhilarating moment, as it validated my knowledge and preparedness. While I acknowledge that my journey through the application process and exam may have been smoother than anticipated, I am aware that others may face different challenges. Each individual's experience is unique, and it is essential to recognize and support those who may encounter additional hurdles along the way.

For those who find themselves in a similar position, I would encourage them to seek guidance and support throughout the process. Utilize available resources such as study materials, practice exams, and study groups. Additionally, maintaining a positive mindset and staying motivated can greatly contribute to success. Ultimately, passing the exam on the first attempt was a significant achievement for me. It served as a reminder that hard work and dedication pay off. I am grateful for the knowledge and confidence gained through the process, and I am excited to embark on the next phase of my career as a Board-Certified Behavior Analyst (BCBA).

Upon becoming licensed, I felt confident in my clinical abilities but recognized a weakness in my administrative skills. The lack of practice in writing comprehensive reports, treatment plans, and other administrative tasks during my training became apparent. Thankfully, I was fortunate enough to learn on the job and receive guidance from my colleagues. This experience highlighted the importance of integrating administrative training alongside clinical practice, ensuring a well-rounded skill set.

From my journey, I've learned valuable lessons that I want to share with others. First and foremost, practicing clinical skills is of utmost importance, especially with challenging cases, while still under close supervision. It is through such practice that we gain confidence and expertise. Furthermore, maintaining strong communication and contact with supervisors is vital even after obtaining licensure. Their guidance and mentorship continue to be valuable resources throughout one's career.

In sharing my story, I hope to inspire others and emphasize the significance of practice, humility, and ongoing support. No matter how skilled we become, it is essential to recognize that we never truly know it all. Everyone, especially during the initial stages of their career, requires support and guidance. By fostering a culture of continuous learning and collaboration, we can create a stronger and more compassionate community within our profession.

Marina L, MSW

In my pursuit of higher education, I dedicated three years to completing my graduate program in international social work. Initially, my dream was to become a psychologist, but along the way, I discovered that I could provide therapy as a social worker. Intrigued by this possibility, I enrolled in a social work program, only to realize that to specialize as a school social worker, I needed to invest an additional six months of study. The coursework covered a wide range of topics, including local and global issues and policies, but it left me yearning for a deeper understanding of clinical practice.

During my time in graduate school, I embarked on two distinct internships that broadened my perspective. The first took place at a detention center, where I honed my skills in case management. The second internship immersed me in the dynamic environment of a school, exposing me to the challenges faced by students. While my program aimed to provide a comprehensive understanding of social work, I felt that it fell short in terms of preparing me to become a skilled clinician.

Although my graduate program lacked the mentorship and guidance I craved, I was fortunate to have a supervisor who also served as a professor. Under his tutelage, I had the opportunity to participate in clinical groups and sessions, gaining valuable experience. Despite this, I still lacked the confidence to apply for jobs in schools, feeling ill-equipped for the challenges that lay ahead.

Taking a temporary detour, I ventured into the world of yoga instruction after graduation. While teaching yoga brought me joy, my passion for social work and the desire to provide therapy persisted within me. However, the daunting process of applying for licensure has caused me to delay completion for the past ten years. Although I have amassed the necessary hours, the complexities of the application process have left me feeling overwhelmed. Nevertheless, I remain determined to complete it this year, carefully considering the pros and cons that come with becoming licensed.

Reflecting on my experiences, I have come to understand that a professional license does not automatically guarantee the quality of one's work. Sadly, I have witnessed fully licensed clinicians who deliver subpar services. This realization underscores the importance of ongoing learning, professional development, and a commitment to honing our skills beyond licensure. However, despite the limitations, I still believe that obtaining an LCSW/LCPC license can enhance professional credibility and open doors to new opportunities.

As I continue to navigate my professional journey, I recognize that education is merely the starting point of my growth as a clinician. Real-world experience, continuous learning, and seeking guidance from mentors outside of formal programs are pivotal in my ongoing development. I am resolute in investing in my personal growth, pursuing professional development opportunities, and fostering connections with mentors who can provide guidance and support. By doing so, I am confident that I will continue to evolve as a social worker and provide exceptional care to those I serve.

My message to others is this: Obtaining a professional license, like an LCSW/LCPC, does not guarantee that someone is a good clinician. Licensure is not the sole measure of competence. What truly matters is a commitment to ongoing learning, self-improvement, and a genuine passion for helping others. Exceptional clinicians prioritize continuous growth, seek mentorship, and constantly strive to improve their abilities. Ultimately, it is the quality of care provided and the dedication to client well-being that defines a clinician, regardless of licensure.

SM, LSW

My path to licensure began when I was a freshman in college. Unlike many of my peers in the field, I did not have a passion for helping others from a young age. To be honest, I barely knew anything about therapy, counseling, or the field of mental health for most of my life. It was a topic that was barely discussed within my family, school, or friends, even though it was definitely needed at those times. I remember my freshman year registration, choosing the classes for my first semester. I intended to study Speech Language Pathology at that time. For some unknown reason, I also took Psychology 101 during my first semester. It was during that class that my career path and my life would change. I had always done okay at school but mostly to please my parents and teachers. Taking a psychology course, I found myself interested in the subject like never before in school. When I realized I was as intrigued by an academic course as I was with sports and movies, I knew this was something different and worth exploring further.

That interest led me to pursue a major in Psychology and a minor in Social Work. I began to learn more about the profession and the mental, emotional, and social impacts a social worker can provide. I was fortunate to have a professor who helped teach and develop the skills I continue to use each and every day. This relationship with an undergraduate professor instilled confidence and the motivation to make a change in the community.

By the time I was getting ready to graduate with my undergraduate degree, I knew that I wanted to help others in the capacity that I felt I was able to, which was as a mental health therapist. I had applied to a few Master of Social Work programs and was eager to continue my journey. My MSW program was an intense but eye-opening experience. I am privileged and fortunate to have attended an MSW program with resources, support, and connections. For so long in my life, I had gone to schools and been in communities with people who looked just like me. At this time, I was able to experience a diverse range of people, ideas, and backgrounds that have been instrumental in my learning and development as a social worker. I was lucky enough to have strong support during my MSW program, where I was provided with guidance to help navigate the career field. When I look back on the experience, it reminds me of a successful coach and player in any sport. A successful coach needs to be able to teach and guide a player to obtain what they want, while a player needs to be able to take that knowledge and implement it in a positive way. The staff during my MSW program were great at providing information and answering questions, and it was up to me to take that and run with it.

A part of the MSW program was completing 2 clinical practicums. Many MSW schools place their students into programs, but we had to search, apply, and interview on our own. The school assisted in providing resources and has developed relationships over the years. My first practicum was as a school social worker at a High School in an Urban Midwest city. During my time there, I learned a lot from hands-on experiences. I also was presented with some of the systemic obstacles and issues that are so prevalent in the social work field. Due to low staffing and a high volume of needs, the social worker to student ratio was not healthy. My supervisor was knowledgeable and could handle any situation thrown her way, but unfortunately, many of the issues were out of her control. She was the only social worker for 3 schools in the area, jumping around from school to school, mostly "putting out fires." I was able to witness incredible work ethic and undeniable care for her community. Unfortunately, it was only for a few hours a week, as that was what her schedule allowed for. When I look back on that experience, it reminds me that at times, we as social workers can only do so much.

I graduated with my MSW degree in the spring of 2020 as Covid-19 began. Like many others, I did not have the normal ending to a school year. I knew I wanted to work as a school social worker, as both of my practicum experiences involved a school and I knew that I could make a difference there. I realized that, especially for youth and children, the school setting is one of the first places where support and intervention can occur. I proceeded to work 2 years in a school, which came with many highs and lows. It was not too different from my practicum experience where the number of staff was low, which made it difficult at times for a young social worker. I was at a K-12 school with only one other social worker, in the midst of the Covid-19 pandemic. It was a constant running around trying to solve the next crisis. I remember realizing that I did not feel like I was learning impactful skills that can be transferable in other settings. The support was present but only via email and team meetings every so often. There was barely time to eat lunch, rather have 1:1 supervision. It was time for a change to help my career and my own self-care.

During this time, I obtained my LSW. I was lucky enough that the state of Illinois changed the requirements to obtain an LSW. Instead of having to take an exam, the only criterion was completing the application.

I knew I wanted, at some point, to obtain my LCSW license and realized during my second year at the school that I needed to start making steps to achieve that. I applied to a different job as a Mental Health Therapist in a substance use and mental health setting. In my current job, I am working with a diverse range of clients and concerns. In a little over a year working there, I have learned so much just through the different experiences and situations alone. I have also been guided and supported by appropriate supervision, which has enhanced my learning.

Unlike my experiences in the school system, I have been receiving appropriate supervision. An important piece of that is the ratio of the number of staff members to supervisors. Instead of 1 social worker for 3 schools or multiple grades, the caseload has been manageable in a way that real change can be made. This also means that I have had time to process clinical situations, reflect on decisions, and analyze issues that so often arise. In addition to the time with supervision, my current job has pushed me to pursue other certifications. This has led me to earn a Level 1 Team CBT certification and I am in the process of becoming a Level 2.

Something I try to teach my clients is that we can never plan for every uncomfortable situation that could possibly arise; there are just too many possibilities. What we can focus on is working to feel comfortable being uncomfortable. When I look back at some of the negative experiences I faced in my journey, this often comes to mind. As a social worker, the reality is that we work in a field that is overworked and undervalued in the community. Many of us wear multiple different hats while dealing with society's most complex problems. This was tough to learn and realize as a young social worker, but extremely valuable to my journey. A lesson that I have learned along the way is that even during difficult times in our careers, we are still learning important information. This can be learning about ourselves, various systems we work with, participants we engage with, or about the way we respond to certain situations. In this field, even when times may be tough, we are always learning and getting better. I believe learning does not have to come only from positive experiences but also through the tough times as well.

Currently, I am less than a month away from sitting for the LCSW exam. I have been enjoying going back and reviewing some of the concepts that I learned during my college career. Except this time, I can use firsthand experiences to help reinforce the concepts. I am glad that there is still a part of me that is eager to learn, like when I was sitting in my Psychology 101 class.

Gabriela R. LSW

I graduated from Loyola in 2008 and completed two clinical internships at community agencies, fulfilling all required hours without interruption—one lasting six months and the other a full year. At the first agency, I encountered passive aggression from colleagues who neither instructed me properly nor tolerated mistakes, leading to harsh criticisms. I later discovered they had disparaged me behind my back during a challenging six-month winter stint. My supervisor made inappropriate comments regarding my ethnicity, fostering an environment of institutional mistreatment.

The second agency suffered from poor management characterized by favoritism and dishonest conduct by the supervising manager, who misused his authority. This led to conflicts requiring intervention from my Loyola director to ensure he signed off on my accurately reported and verified hours.

These experiences with inadequate leadership not only undermined my confidence in my suitability for social work but also had detrimental side effects on my life. They left me emotionally and physically strained, resulting in frequent bouts of anxiety, headaches, stomach pains, weight gain, and thyroid issues. The impact of poor leadership extended far beyond professional challenges, deeply affecting my personal health and well-being.

My first job in the field was with an agency specializing in crisis management, where I was supervised by a power-hungry colleague only three years my senior and a fellow Loyola graduate. She displayed clear favoritism towards male team members and failed to provide necessary training or guidance. Instead, she handed me a caseload with no instructions on how to properly fill out specific documents, forcing me to rely on my teammates for help. Her disrespect for the clients was evident as she referred to "poor" people as smelly and would spray Febreze after they left.

The job interview had promised an LCSW supervisor who would oversee my hours, a critical component for my licensure. However, after a year, it became clear this was a false pretense. The supervisor, although an LCSW, ultimately refused to sign off on my hours. This pattern of poor management—where staff could mistreat others without repercussions—was a recurring theme in every position I held. It made me constantly question my ability to continue in social work. Eventually, when confronted after a year of waiting, the supervisor casually mentioned that the agency did not actually offer supervision hours for licensure, suggesting I should seek them externally.

This experience, combined with ongoing management issues, led me to a pivotal decision when my child was born. I chose to leave the professional world to stay home, recognizing that the challenges within my work environments were detracting significantly from my personal well-being and professional integrity. I had entered social work to support and uplift my community, but found myself consistently undermined by the very people who were supposed to be my allies.

After ten years, driven by financial needs and the desire to show my children the importance of education and professional readiness, I felt a spiritual call to return to work. I secured a remote position managing crisis interventions from home, which offered a measure of comfort. This job promised supervision and eventually agreed to pay for private supervision. Despite its organizational flaws and lack of recognition, I managed to practice and enhance my skills. I developed educational newsletters on cultural diversity and mentored new or struggling staff members.

This job has had its own set of challenges, such as favoritism and unfair practices. Yet, the resilience I developed from previous experiences and the remote nature of the work helped me to stay longer than I might have otherwise. I've learned to navigate these challenges effectively, reinforcing my commitment to social work and my ability to make a meaningful impact in my field.

In 2022, I achieved a significant milestone by obtaining my LSW, and I have since submitted my LCSW application, currently awaiting the results. I am proud of how much I have accomplished in the last two years. This success is not because it has been easy, but because I am determined to pursue bigger and better opportunities. I have already interviewed with a promising private practice, and the set of three interviews were amazing, offering new possibilities for growth and development in my career.

Regarding my most recent supervision, which allowed me to accumulate partial clinical hours, my internal supervisor, who was based in another state, was generally supportive and helped me grow in the job. However, she had to adhere to the company's protocols, even when they weren't fair or realistic. It became problematic when individuals without licenses were allowed to supervise shifts, a practice both unfair and unethical. Fortunately, my job agreed to pay for external supervision, which provided the best support I've ever received. My external supervisor's knowledge, support, and encouragement were crucial in building my confidence. This type of supportive environment is what our field needs more of—we need the ability to ask questions without fear. There's a quote that resonates with me deeply: "Your manager has more impact on your mental health than your therapist or your doctor. Having a good boss can literally change your life." This statement is incredibly true, and I hope all newcomers in the field can learn from our experiences and find leadership that empowers and prepares them for greater things.

My Advice: Always keep a tracker for your clinical hours and Continuing Education Units (CEUs). It will keep you focused and organized. In this field, it's crucial not to trust too quickly or assume that everyone has your best interests at heart. While the profession is dedicated to helping others, not everyone may uphold these principles. Despite these challenges, never give up on searching for your place in this field. There's always something new to explore, and a niche where you can truly make a difference and find personal fulfillment. Persist in your journey, and you'll discover your own "happy place" within the behavioral health field.

Stories End

I deeply appreciate the profound lessons embedded within these stories, recognizing their immense value in shaping your preparation for the licensing journey. The inherent power of these narratives lies in their ability to serve as guiding lights, endowing you with invaluable insights and empowering you to navigate the inevitable challenges that may arise. The wisdom encapsulated within these tales resonates with me, and I hold it in high regard.

By immersing yourself in these stories, you gain a holistic understanding of the licensing journey. The challenges presented at different stages provide you with a heads-up for the various settings you are likely to encounter. This knowledge allows you to approach each stage with a prepared mindset, equipped with the tools necessary to overcome obstacles and thrive.

Furthermore, these stories not only offer practical guidance but also nurture your ability to think critically and adapt. They encourage you to develop a flexible mindset, recognizing that each licensing experience may present unique challenges requiring different strategies and approaches.

Embrace the lessons the stories offered and reflect upon how they can be applied to your own licensing journey. Extract the key principles and insights, and let them guide your decision-making and actions.

❖ Challenges walk alongside opportunities for growth.

❖ Growth walks alongside pain.

❖ Endings walk alongside new possibilities.

Chapter 7: Beyond Licensure

After completing the licensing process, it is crucial to prioritize lifelong learning and professional growth. Obtaining a license does not signify the end of professional development; rather, it necessitates ongoing training to maintain compliance and ethics. I encourage you to explore opportunities for specialization and identify the therapy approach that aligns with your passion and desired expertise. Finding your specialization depends on exposing yourself to various clinical approaches.

Personally, I have discovered certain modalities that I feel comfortable implementing in my practice, disregarding external pressures or demands for specific therapy approaches. While I continue to receive further training to enhance my skills, I focus on sharpening my expertise within my chosen approaches rather than adding new ones. While having multiple specializations is acceptable, true specialization requires ongoing practice. I recommend searching for a therapy approach that resonates with you and enrolling in a certification program. If you are still in graduate school and have determined your preferred therapy approach, taking advantage of student discounts can be beneficial.

During my time in graduate school, I made the strategic decision to pursue certification and specialization, which allowed me to save over 50% of the tuition fee. To this day, I continue to draw upon the knowledge gained from that specialization in my therapy sessions, recognizing its profound impact on my practice. I am committed to ongoing professional development and actively engage in training programs and take meticulous notes to stay abreast of the latest advancements in the field.

Although I hold multiple certifications as a result of work requirements, I consider myself specialized in just four approaches: Enneagram, Integrative Mental Health, Perinatal Mood and Anxiety Disorders and Rapid Resolution Therapy. Throughout a 10+ year journey, I have dedicated myself to becoming the best version of myself by maintaining a strong connection to training opportunities, actively participating in the therapy community, and staying informed about the latest updates and research in the field. This continuous pursuit of growth and excellence allows me to provide the highest quality of care to my clients and ensures that I remain at the forefront of my profession.

Let's go over some key points:

1. Embrace Lifelong Learning: Always be open to new knowledge and skills throughout your career as a therapist.

2. Explore Specialization: Identify therapy approaches that resonate with you and commit to mastering your chosen modality.

3. Diverse Clinical Exposure: Actively participate in workshops and seminars to explore different therapies. Consider experiencing therapy from the client's perspective to deeply understand its impact and integrate valuable insights into your practice.

4. Follow Your Instincts: Choose therapy approaches that align with your values and feel right for your practice, rather than following trends.

5. Pursue Advanced Training: Seek specialized certification in your preferred modality to deepen your expertise.

6. Leverage Student Discounts: If you're still studying, take advantage of student discounts for certifications to build expertise early and economically.

7. Practice Continuously: Regularly apply and refine the techniques you learn to keep your skills sharp.

8. Stay Informed and Connected: Engage with your professional community, keep up with the latest research, and participate in forums and discussions to remain current in your field.

9. Maintain a CEU Tracker: Use a tracker to organize and monitor your Continuing Education Units to ensure you meet professional development requirements.

10. Maintain a CEU Tracker: Keeping track of Continuing Education Units (CEUs) is essential for professional development. A CEU tracker helps you stay organized and ensures you meet the necessary requirements for maintaining your credentials and/or certifications.

Remember, it takes time and dedication to become specialized in a therapy approach. Focus on mastering a few approaches rather than trying to be a jack-of-all-trades. Regardless of your specific license, all licenses will require mandatory Continuing Education Units (CEUs), so choose your CEUs wisely to align with your specialization and professional goals. By continuously investing in your professional growth and selecting relevant CEUs, you can become the best version of yourself as a therapist.

❖ *Self-compassion walks alongside nurturing oneself with kindness.*

❖ *Experience walks alongside wisdom.*

❖ *Boundaries walk alongside protecting one's well-being.*

Chapter 8: The One Case

For reasons of confidentiality, I named this case Angel. The journey with Angel was not just a case for me; it was a turning point in my career, a case that changed my life forever. It opened my eyes to the harsh reality of how clients are often seen as mere numbers in the system. It also revealed the struggles faced by clinicians within the non-profit sector, where they can lose themselves in the bureaucratic systems and lose sight of the needs of the individuals they serve.

In the realm of our profession, I had often been told that there would come a defining case—one that would either uplift and fortify me or shatter my resolve entirely. My grad school professors had imparted this wisdom, emphasizing the transformative power that a single case can hold. Little did I know that I would encounter such a case—one that would simultaneously build me up and test my limits, unveiling strengths and vulnerabilities I never thought possible.

Angel's story would unfold in ways that defied all expectations, leaving an indelible mark on my professional and personal life. It was a case that defied conventional boundaries and surpassed anything I had ever encountered. As I delved deeper into Angel's world, I soon realized that this was no ordinary case—it was a profound catalyst for transformation. The agency within which I operated often succumbed to the harsh realities of the system, reducing clients to mere statistics and losing sight of their humanity. Yet, in the presence of Angel, the walls of detachment crumbled, leaving me no choice but to reassess the very essence of my role as a clinician and the profound influence I could wield in the lives of those I served.

In the face of bureaucratic obstacles and institutional limitations, I witnessed firsthand the immense struggles faced by Angel. Their journey became my own, and I was determined to navigate the intricate web of systems that threatened to suffocate their individuality and needs. It was a daunting task, one that would push me to my limits and challenge the very core of who I was as a clinician. But within the depths of this complex case, I discovered unexpected reservoirs of strength and resilience. The adversities we faced became stepping stones for growth, propelling me to defy conventional boundaries and reimagine the possibilities of my profession. I resolved to be the unwavering advocate that Angel needed, forging connections and delving into unfamiliar territories to ensure their voice was heard.

As I ventured into uncharted territory, I found myself immersed in the study of American Sign Language, determined to bridge the communication gap and truly understand Angel's unique perspective. Through this journey of learning and adaptation, a profound therapeutic relationship took root—one built on trust, understanding, and genuine connection. Angel became more than just a client; they became a beacon of inspiration and an embodiment of resilience. However, as Angel's situation reached critical levels, I discovered that the path I believed to be right clashed with the clinical leadership's perspective. Doubt began to seep in, questioning my decisions and stirring the fear of potential failure. Yet, in the face of adversity, I held onto the unwavering belief in Angel's potential and their right to a brighter future.

Driven by my convictions, I sought external support and allies who recognized the significance of Angel's journey. Together, we fought to ensure that Angel's needs were met, advocating tirelessly for their well-being and the transformational environment they deserved. It was a battle that challenged my resilience and perseverance, but one that I could not afford to lose. In the end, Angel's remarkable transformation stood as a testament to the power of resilience and the significance of providing the right support. Witnessing their newfound happiness and the blossoming of their authentic self was a bittersweet triumph. While I reveled in their success, it also served as a stark reminder of the flaws within the system—an agency that failed to acknowledge the magnitude of Angel's journey and the profound impact it had on me as a clinician.

When I first crossed paths with Angel, their circumstances were undeniably dire. Angel was deaf, a condition that persists to this day, and the absence of a dedicated interpreter rendered them incapable of effectively expressing needs and emotions. As a result, their mental health rapidly declined, leading to self-mutilation and multiple suicide attempts. It was heartbreaking to witness the pain Angel was going through, and I knew I had to do something to help. Feeling overwhelmed and unsure where to start, I made the decision to learn American Sign Language (ASL).

Astonishingly, I was able to pick it up quickly, and within a few months, I was communicating with Angel directly. The ability to connect on a deeper level was transformative. I became the safe space, the person they could rely on and confide in. However, my dedication to Angel's well-being began to raise eyebrows among my colleagues and staff. They questioned my boundaries, concerned that I was taking on too much responsibility and risking my own mental health. I couldn't turn my back on Angel. I knew that being their advocate was essential for their recovery. At certain points, Angel's case reached a state of daily crisis, where even the smallest triggers could set off a distressing response.

I vividly recall the traumatic day when I witnessed Angel attempting suicide. Angel expressed a desire to go for a walk, using sign language to convey the need for fresh air. Despite Angel's plea, the agency denied them the opportunity due to a lack of available staff. In my limited ASL proficiency, I tried to reassure Angel and redirect their focus to other matters. However, I will never forget the moment when Angel signed to me, "I will choke myself, I just want to die." In an instant, Angel dashed to the top bunk bed, swiftly transforming a bedsheet into a makeshift rope. It all happened so quickly, like a blur of motion. Angel tightly wrapped the improvised rope around their neck and hands, made a nod pulling with an alarming determination. I was in disbelief, in shock as I witnessed this unfolding tragedy.

Desperately, I screamed for help while trying to reach Angel, with half of my body suspended in mid-air and the other half on the top bunk bed. As I screamed out for assistance, Angel continued to pull on the rope, their face transitioning from red to pale and eventually to a haunting shade of purple. I will never forget the anguish in Angel's eyes—a profound yearning for death and an unimaginable amount of pain. Then, suddenly, Angel's eyes rolled back, turning completely white, as they lost consciousness.

Help arrived, but even then, they struggled to release the rope constricting Angel's neck. My vision was blurred, and my hearing became muffled in the aftermath of witnessing this traumatic event. A compassionate colleague was tasked with escorting me to my office, where I attempted to find solace and sobbed uncontrollably, my thoughts consumed by the uncertainty of Angel's fate. In that moment, I couldn't escape the haunting feeling that Angel had slipped away before my eyes. The staff provided unwavering support and stood beside me, offering great comfort during this challenging ordeal. Finally, Angel was escorted to my office by the paramedics, and in that profound moment, their eyes expressed a profound sense of remorse, silently conveying a message before their hands moved to sign, "I am sorry."

This deeply distressing experience remains burned into my memory, a constant reminder of the fragility of life and the profound impact of our work as clinicians. It underscores the urgent need for mental health support, compassion, and proactive intervention in situations of crisis. It is a stark reminder of the resilience of the human spirit and the critical importance of being attuned to the cries for help that may be hidden behind silent suffering.

Sadly, this was not the last in a series of distressing events, as Angel's journey continued to be marked by hardships and challenges. The severity of their situation necessitated frequent calls to 911 for immediate assistance. The ER staff, witnessing the recurring nature of the crisis, recognized that the root cause lay within the agency itself rather than with Angel. Consequently, they involved the Department of Children and Family Services (DCFS) to address the systemic issues at play. The sheer extent of external involvement, including emergency services and child welfare authorities, was unparalleled in my professional experience.

Navigating through these intricate dynamics and coordinating with multiple sources posed an immense challenge that required unwavering commitment and resilience. Additionally, the demands of this case pushed me to write an extensive number of clinical notes, reports, and emails. As a result, my writing skills were honed and improved significantly throughout this process. As Angel's situation reached a critical point, I fought tooth and nail to prevent them from being transferred to a long-term treatment center. The upper leadership, unfortunately, insisted on it. Determined to protect Angel, I reached out to external sources for help. Fortunately, they listened to my pleas and understood the urgency of the situation. Together, we managed to find the right placement where Angel could be part of a supportive community instead of being isolated but this process took months.

By this point the toll on my own mental health was undeniable. I questioned my judgment, wondering if I was lacking in boundaries or experiencing secondary trauma, compassion fatigue, or burnout. The doubts threatened to drown out my voice, but I persevered because I knew that Angel's well-being hung in the balance as the truth revealed that the entire agency was engulfed in chaos, unsure of how to handle this particular case. Due to my resistance with clinical leadership, Angel was repeatedly transferred to different therapists in a desperate search for one who would endorse a long-term inpatient unit that lacked appropriate services for the deaf. Even after I was no longer their therapist, Angel sought answers and validation from me. I reassured them that they had done nothing wrong and reminded Angel of the positive changes that were ahead.

Then, in early spring of the following year, Angel burst into my office, radiating pure happiness and excitement. I distinctly remember putting aside my LCSW study binder, fully immersing myself in the moment, and giving Angel my undivided attention. Excitedly, Angel shared the news of acceptance into a deaf school, where they would finally be surrounded by the deaf community. Although I had already been informed of Angel's acceptance by external sources, I understood that it was my responsibility to maintain confidentiality and honor the integrity of the process that needed to unfold in its own time.

As we watched the recording of Angel's school interview, capturing their genuine joy and the promising future that awaited in the beautiful environment, a whirlwind of emotions washed over me. I couldn't help but feel an overwhelming sense of happiness for Angel's incredible opportunity, but simultaneously, a surge of anger welled up inside me directed at the upper clinical leadership team for depriving me of the chance to be involved in the most rewarding phase of the case. Those six minutes felt agonizingly long, and as Angel left my office, tears streamed down my face, unable to contain the overwhelming emotions within me. In that vulnerable moment, I sought solace in confiding in a supportive coworker, sharing my realization that my true purpose within the agency was to provide unwavering support to Angel and ensure they were placed in the most suitable environment for their growth and well-being. It was a deeply profound understanding that reaffirmed my commitment to advocating for the individuals I serve, even in the face of challenges and opposition.

It was then that the idea of writing about Angel's case took hold. I knew that their journey had to be shared, and my experiences and emotions needed an outlet. As I poured my heart and soul into writing, the paragraphs and sentences flowed effortlessly. Writing became a way for me to process my own feelings, reflect on the lessons learned, and give voice to Angel's struggles. Despite the challenges and the lack of recognition from the agency, I found solace in knowing that Angel was safe, regulated, and hopeful for the future.

Through this experience, I learned invaluable lessons. I learned that empathy among clinicians is not always a given and that we must strive to support and uplift each other. I learned the importance of advocating for clients, even in the face of adversity. I discovered the power of perseverance and the strength that comes from standing up for what is right. And most importantly, I realized that true success lies in the positive impact we have on the lives of those we serve.

Today, Angel's story continues to inspire and touch the hearts of many. News outlets have highlighted their remarkable journey, celebrating their achievements and the positive impact Angel has made in the community.

Angel has become a symbol of resilience and determination, proving that with the right support and opportunities, anyone can overcome adversity and thrive. Angel's newfound happiness radiates through every aspect of their lives. Angel excels academically, immersing themselves in their studies and embracing the rich educational environment of the deaf school.

Surrounded by peers who understand and appreciate their unique experiences, Angel has found a sense of belonging and acceptance that they had longed for. Not only has Angel succeeded academically, but they have also discovered their passion for sports. Through their creative expressions, Angel communicates emotions, dreams, and hopes to the world. Angel's commitment to sports has gained recognition and has been shown in videos, touching the hearts of those who view them. Angel has become a beacon of hope, proving that no matter the obstacles we face, resilience and determination can lead us to a brighter future.

As for me, Angel's story remains etched in my heart and mind. Their journey has reminded me of the transformative power of compassion, advocacy, and the human spirit. It has reaffirmed my commitment to making a difference in the lives of those I serve, and it has taught me the profound impact that one person can have on another. Angel's story is a testament to the resilience and strength that reside within all of us. It serves as a reminder that no matter the challenges we encounter, there is always hope for a brighter tomorrow.

The truth is, Angel's case involved many individuals, and I acknowledge that each person may have their own perspective and lessons learned from it. Throughout this journey, I experienced both support and opposition, making friends and enemies along the way. While there are diverse viewpoints, I choose to hold onto my own perception, as it is through my lens that I witnessed the profound impact of this experience. Every time I reflect on Angel's case, I uncover new lessons that bring a smile to my face. It serves as a powerful reminder of the resilience and strength of the human spirit, highlighting the transformative potential of empathy and compassion in effecting meaningful change.

The insights and knowledge I gained from this case have continued to shape my approach and deepen my understanding of the intricate complexities within our field. I am immensely grateful for the opportunity to have played a role in Angel's story, as it has left a lasting impact on me. The lessons I learned from this experience now serve as guiding principles in my work.

With each new case I encounter, I view it as a chance for growth and the potential for fresh insights. I approach these cases with an open heart and an eagerness to learn. It is through this mindset that I have been able to navigate the diverse challenges and celebrate the triumphs of being a clinician.

Reflecting on Angel's case, I find solace in the knowledge that I have grown, evolved, and become an even stronger advocate for those in need. One important lesson I learned is that institutional trauma is a real issue, and sometimes, unintentionally, we can become part of the problem. It was not until I found myself in that situation that I fully understood the meaning behind my professor's statement: "If you see a problem and you do not say anything, you then become part of the problem."

The realization of my own involvement in perpetuating the problem led me to speak up and remove myself from it, even if it meant enduring the consequences. This experience has reinforced my commitment to being a responsible and ethical clinician, and it has taught me the importance of actively challenging and addressing systemic issues to create positive change.

For the sake of maintaining the same format, I will list the valuable lessons I learned through this transformative experience.

Here are some key lessons to consider:

1. The Power of Advocacy: I discovered the immense importance of advocating fiercely for the well-being and best interests of my clients, even in the face of opposition. I realized that sometimes I had to go beyond the boundaries of my role to ensure that their voices were heard, and their needs were met.

2. The Impact of Building Relationships: This case showed me the profound impact of establishing genuine and empathetic relationships with clients. By taking the time to learn American Sign Language and becoming Angel's trusted confidant, I witnessed firsthand the positive effects it had on his mental health and overall well-being.

3. The Realities of Bureaucracy: I was confronted with the harsh reality of how clients can be reduced to mere numbers within the bureaucratic systems of non-profit organizations. It taught me the importance of navigating these systems while maintaining a client-centered focus, always prioritizing their needs above administrative protocols.

4. The Strength in Emotional Resilience: This case pushed me to the limits of my emotional resilience. It challenged me to confront my doubts and fears and the noise surrounding me, yet I found the inner strength to persevere and stay true to my convictions.

5. The Value of Self-Reflection and Self-Care: Angel's case emphasized the importance of self-reflection and self-care when confronted with overwhelming circumstances. It became evident that, in order to effectively support my clients, I must prioritize my own well-being. This includes regularly engaging in self-reflection to assess my emotional and mental state, as well as evaluating my boundaries to ensure they are healthy and sustainable. Recognizing signs of burnout, compassion fatigue, or secondary trauma is crucial, and taking proactive steps to address them is essential for maintaining personal well-being and providing quality care to those I serve. Through this experience, I learned that self-care is not a luxury but a necessity, enabling me to show up as the best version of myself in my professional role.

6. The Inequalities Within the Field: This experience shed light on the inequalities that exist within the field of mental health, including the disparity between

credentials and actual competence. It motivated me to continuously enhance my knowledge, skills, and ethical understanding to ensure the best possible care for my clients.

7. The Power of Perseverance: Angel's case taught me the importance of perseverance in the face of adversity. Despite numerous obstacles and setbacks, I witnessed firsthand the resilience of the human spirit. It reinforced the need to persistently advocate for those in need, never giving up on finding the right solutions and support.

8. The Impact of Effective Communication: Angel's struggle to communicate due to the lack of an interpreter highlighted the profound impact that effective communication can have on an individual's well-being. It emphasized the significance of providing accessible communication tools and resources to ensure individuals can express their needs, emotions, and experiences fully.

9. The Role of Empathy and Compassion: Witnessing Angel's pain and journey deepened my understanding of the vital role empathy and compassion play in our work. It reminded me to approach everyone with empathy, seeking to understand their unique experiences and providing a safe and supportive space for them to heal and grow.

10. The Value of Reflective Practice: Reflecting on Angel's case allowed me to uncover new insights and lessons along the way. It underscored the importance of engaging in reflective practice, continually evaluating

my actions, decisions, and interventions, and learning from them to enhance my professional practice.

11. The Power of Personal Growth: Angel's journey served as a catalyst for my personal growth as a clinician. It challenged me to expand my skills, deepen my knowledge, and refine my approach to better serve those I work with. It reminded me that personal growth is an ongoing process that evolves with each new experience.

As I continue my professional journey, the valuable lessons learned from Angel's case serve as an enduring reminder, guiding my practice and strengthening my commitment to fostering positive change. This particular case led me to encounter the CEO of Deaf Defy, a non-profit organization dedicated to supporting deaf children. It opened my eyes to a previously unknown need, and since then, I have actively supported Deaf Defy.

While I wish I could provide you with all the necessary tools to handle challenging cases, I acknowledge that this is beyond my capacity. Nonetheless, I feel compelled to write this heartfelt letter, recognizing that every case you will encounter is unique and unpredictable.

Dear Fellow Professional,

I hope this letter finds you well as you embark on your professional journey. In our chosen fields, we encounter various complexities, and I wanted to take a moment to stress the significance of familiarizing oneself with the code of ethics that governs our work. This code serves as a moral compass, guiding us through intricate situations.

Amidst challenges and tough decisions, I encourage you to trust your instincts and intuition, for they often lead us to what is right and just. Upholding ethical principles demands courage and conviction, particularly in the face of adversity. Stand strong and unwavering in your beliefs, knowing that your commitment to integrity will shape your professional path.

Continuous expansion of knowledge and expertise is crucial for making a positive difference in the lives of those we serve. Embrace opportunities to learn and grow, seeking out new perspectives and remaining dedicated to ongoing development. By doing so, you equip yourself with the necessary tools to navigate the ever-changing landscape of our professions and contribute to the advancement of our field.

Remain true to your values, expand your knowledge, and strive to be a compassionate and competent professional. The impact you have on those you serve is immeasurable, and your dedication to ethical practice will set you apart in your field. Don't hesitate to address your supervisors, even when they are entangled in the politics of the field.

May your journey be characterized by continuous growth, meaningful impact, and personal fulfillment. Stay steadfast in your dedication to ethical practice and let it guide you towards professional excellence. Through your commitment and expertise, you possess the potential to make a significant and positive difference in the world. Let us always prioritize a client-centered approach rather than being solely program-centered. Let us remember that our clients are more than just numbers or meeting grant requirements.

Wishing you all the best on your journey.

Sincerely,

Xiomara Ramirez, LCSW, CADC, CIMHP

Conclusion

The licensing process for aspiring professionals in our field is in dire need of reevaluation. Accepting hardship as a norm within our profession should not be tolerated. We must strive for a licensing process that fosters well-being, support, and growth. This book has explored the myriad challenges and considerations that arise during the transition from graduate school to professional practice, offering personal experiences, practical advice, and insights to empower you on your journey.

I've emphasized the importance of meticulous planning and attention to detail in the license application process. By learning from past experiences and staying informed, you can navigate this complex process with greater confidence. Proper preparation for the licensing exam is crucial, and the tools and insights provided here aim to help you approach these challenges effectively.

Supervision and mentorship are essential in enhancing clinical skills and professional growth, particularly during the first 15-20 years of practice. Engaging in therapy aids in personal growth and well-being, helping us process life's challenges and improve the care we provide to our clients. Continuous professional development through supervision and continuing education is key to advancing your clinical expertise.

As the field evolves, so do therapy approaches. Remain open-minded and curious. There is much to learn, and limiting yourself to one job or area can prevent you from fully leveraging your education and experiences. Explore various therapy approaches, pursue additional training, and engage actively with the behavioral health community to continuously enhance your expertise.

Lastly, remember to focus on your own growth and ignore workplace negativity. Co-workers who indulge in gossip and negativity often reflect their own dissatisfaction. By concentrating on your advancement, you can avoid being dragged into bitterness. Some may not be interested in improving the environment and might even take pleasure in seeing others struggle. However, let's aim to be the generation that breaks this cycle, fostering a more supportive and positive work environment for all.

Your Journey Towards Licensing

Share your inspiring licensing journey by emailing it to xio@forward-hope.com. Together, we can create a tapestry of triumph and resilience that helps guide and support others in our field. Your story can provide practical insights and encouragement to newcomers, helping them navigate similar challenges more effectively. I look forward to celebrating and sharing your unique experiences as we build a community that learns and grows together.

Writing this book has highlighted the significant impact that unaddressed challenges can have on clinicians. Addressing and openly discussing these issues is crucial for creating a supportive environment that promotes healing and professional growth. By sharing these experiences, we aim to enhance understanding and prepare future clinicians for the realities of the profession.

If you're encountering difficulties related to your journey toward licensing, consider the importance of professional mentorship or support. Receiving guidance can help you manage and overcome these challenges, allowing you to develop into a well-qualified and resilient professional. Remember, prioritizing your well-being and seeking assistance are positive steps towards personal growth and professional excellence.

Embrace Your Passion

If you've ever dreamed of writing a book or pursuing a passion, I encourage you to seize the opportunity! Let go of doubts and embrace the journey ahead. As I began my book-writing endeavor, the adventure unfolded naturally, with each step bringing the pieces together. Allow your faith and spirit to guide you, letting creativity flow. This approach is valid for any aspiration—take that first brave step and watch your journey unfold, aiming to become the best version of yourself.

Don't let fears and insecurities hold you back. At times, I doubted my qualifications, wondering if I had enough experience to write a book. Yet, I realized that it's not the length but the quality and depth of your experiences that count. Everyone has unique insights and lessons that are valuable to others.

So, let your passion lead you, trust in your abilities, and express your creativity. Your voice matters, your story is worth telling, and your journey is worth pursuing. Embrace the unknown, for it holds the magic of self-discovery and fulfillment. I wish you inspiration and success in all your endeavors. Thank you for joining me on this literary journey, and I hope it has positively impacted your path to licensing.

Honoring the Silent Stories

This final page is dedicated to those who have felt hindered by fear, shame, and guilt in sharing their stories. I understand the emotions tied to untold narratives and empathize with your struggles. I've received messages from many expressing feelings like, "I'm scared," "I'm embarrassed," and "I thought I was the only one struggling." Your honesty underscores our shared challenges and the importance of this book. Thank you for your trust.

Life's experiences can make us feel vulnerable and pressured to remain silent. Acknowledging the immense courage it takes to even consider sharing, I recognize that the decision to keep your story private is deeply personal. However, the burden of silence does not diminish your story's significance.

Let this dedication validate the unseen stories. You are not alone. May you find comfort in knowing your voice matters, your story matters.

About the Author

Xiomara Ramirez is a highly dedicated and accomplished professional, fueled by a profound passion for assisting others. She founded Forward Hope, LLC, a remote private practice dedicated to offering holistic approaches to mental health and wellbeing. Xiomara's professional journey is marked by her diverse roles, including clinical director, clinical supervisor, field instructor, substance use counselor, migration and trauma therapist, infant-toddler specialist, and family support specialist. Currently, she contributes her expertise to the State of Illinois, continuing her commitment to making a positive impact.

With a master's degree from Loyola University School of Social Work and a Certified Alcohol and Drug Counselor (CADC) qualification, Xiomara possesses a strong educational foundation and extensive expertise. She has further expanded her knowledge by obtaining a graduate-level certification as an Infant Toddler Specialist from Erikson Institute, demonstrating her commitment to early childhood development. Xiomara is registered as a qualified Clinical Supervisor with the National

Association of Social Workers (NASW), exemplifying her dedication to maintaining professional standards and providing mentorship in the field. Additionally, she serves as the Secretary on the Board of Loyola School of Social Work Alumni and as a student mentor.

Her recent certification as an Enneagram Instructor further demonstrates her commitment to understanding individual differences and fostering personal growth. Xiomara firmly believes in the value of understanding and respecting different personality styles, recognizing the importance of tailoring her approach to meet their unique needs.

As an Integrative Mental Health Professional, Xiomara strives to deliver comprehensive and holistic care to her clients. She acknowledges the significance of addressing mental health from a multidimensional perspective and integrates various therapeutic approaches and practices into her work.

With over a decade of experience in fields such as children and families, behavioral health, migration, and trauma, she possesses a wealth of knowledge and expertise. Her dedication to community service is evident through her ten years of volunteer work in the faith-recovery community, where she currently hosts free online groups in English and Spanish providing invaluable support and guidance to those in need.

In her pursuit of professional growth, Xiomara has obtained several certifications, reflecting her commitment to expanding her skills and knowledge. These certifications include Holistic Mental Health Coach,

Trauma-Informed Practitioner, Perinatal Mental Health, Domestic Violence, Medical Interpreter, Cognitive Behavioral Therapy (CBT) Practitioner, TF-CBT (Trauma-Focused Cognitive Behavioral Therapy), and Rapid Resolution Therapist (RRT).

Xiomara's personal philosophy revolves around continuous learning, teamwork, and hard work. She embraces the idea of approaching life with curiosity and a willingness to learn from every experience. Her favorite quotes, such as "Always walk through life as if you have something new to learn and you will" by Vernon Howard, "Do the best you can until you know better. Then when you know better, do better" by Maya Angelou, "Alone we can do so little; together we can do so much" by Helen Keller, and "Integrity is more valuable than income" by Robin Sharma exemplify her values and belief in personal growth, empathy, and collaboration.

Xiomara's vast expertise, genuine care for others, and commitment to ongoing learning make her a valuable asset in guiding individuals towards personal growth and well-being.

Made in the USA
Monee, IL
12 October 2024

67135153R20079